THE SEARCH FOR TRUTH ABOUT ISLAM

THE SEARCH
FOR TRUTH ABOUT ISLAM

A Christian Pastor Separates Fact from Fiction

BEN DANIEL

WESTMINSTER
JOHN KNOX PRESS
LOUISVILLE · KENTUCKY

First edition
Published by Westminster John Knox Press
Louisville, Kentucky

13 14 15 16 17 18 19 20 21 22—10 9 8 7 6 5 4 3 2 1

Book design by Erika Lundbom
Cover design by designpointinc.com

Library of Congress Cataloging-in-Publication Data

Daniel, Ben.
   The search for truth about Islam : a Christian pastor separates fact from fiction / Ben Daniel. -- 1st ed.
      p. cm.
   Includes bibliographical references and index.
   ISBN 978-0-664-23705-9 (alk. paper)
   1. Islam. 2. Islam--History. 3. Islam--United States. 4. Islamophobia--United States. I. Title.
   BP161.3.D367 2013
   297—dc23

                                                        2012032986

Most Westminster John Knox Press books are available at special quantity discounts when purchased in bulk by corporations, organizations, and special-interest groups. For more information, please e-mail SpecialSales@wjkbooks.com.

For my children, with love:

Miriam LiMing Daniel
Helena QiongLi Daniel
William Johann Daniel

May they inherit a less fearful, more peaceable world.

Those who write have to see that each man's knowledge is, as near as they can make it, answerable to the facts of life; that he shall not suppose himself an angel or a monster; nor take this world for a hell; nor be suffered to imagine that all rights are concentrated in his own caste or country, or all veracities in his own parochial creed.

—Robert Louis Stevenson, "The Morality
of the Profession of Letters," 1881

CONTENTS

Part 3: History

Part 4: Misconceptions

Part 5: The American Cult of Fear

ACKNOWLEDGMENTS

I STARTED THINKING ABOUT *THE SEARCH FOR TRUTH ABOUT ISLAM* during the summer of 2009, as I was finishing a book on immigration. By June 2012 I was finished writing the tome you now hold in your hands. It was an exciting and slightly confusing time to be writing about Islam because so much happened relative to Islam during the gestation of this book. As the United States' military—both overtly and covertly—waged war in at least five predominantly Muslim countries (Iraq, Afghanistan, Pakistan, Yemen, and Libya), acts of terror—both successful and not—were committed in the name of Islam. Prisoners remained in Guantanamo without trial. A progressive Muslim organization made plans to build a community center in lower Manhattan, but fearful pundits accused them of blasphemy and excoriated them as radical terrorists. The Homeland Security Committee of the United States House of Representatives held hearings on radical Islam.[1]

And then there came an Arab Spring, when protestors fed up with totalitarian regimes—many of them supported by the United States—took to the streets and, on a couple of occasions, were successful in ousting dictators. Through it all, dozens of friends, colleagues, and relatives sent me ideas and tips, some of which found their way into the book. For that I am grateful.

During the process of making this book a reality, I have enjoyed support, help, and encouragement from Maha ElGenaidi, the founder and executive director of Islamic Networks Group. She has been generous with her time, her intellect, and her address book. I am thankful.

I am indebted as well to Samir Laymoun, a lay leader in the Muslim Community Association of the San Francisco Bay Area, who has offered sustaining friendship and insight as I thought through ideas for this book.

Professor John Eby of Loras College in Dubuque, Iowa, helped me to distill ideas for my chapters dealing with Córdoba, the Crusades, and the Cathar wars. Geoff Browning gave me ideas for my chapter on Islam and women. Professor Jim Bennett of Santa Clara University was constantly available to confirm or correct my ideas about American religious history. The Rev. John Chamberlain kept me honest by encouraging me to stay active in ecumenical dialogue. Tony and Jackie DeRose were kind enough to listen as I read bits of this book to them.

When an odd twist of circumstance led me to Scotland to learn about Protestant and Catholic sectarian soccer hooliganism while writing a book on Islam (see chapter 7), my kindhearted friends Craig and Michelle Smith of East Kilbride took me into their home. They fed me haggis while reciting Burns. They took me to the castle where Monty Python filmed the Holy Grail. They prayed with me at St. Giles church in Edinburgh. They led me—on increasingly wobbly legs—on a tour of Glasgow's finest pubs. They introduced me to their beautiful circle of family and friends, and together we laughed until our sides hurt. *Alba gu bràth* (Scotland forever), dear friends.

Tahir Anwar, Ray from Bill's Market, Imam Zaid Shakir, Hatem Bazian, Ingrid Mattson, and the above-mentioned Maha ElGenaidi all were kind enough to talk to me about this book on record. I am particularly grateful to Rumiana Nuseibeh of Amman, Jordan, who, upon receipt of an e-mail from a complete stranger, gave me contact information for her brother-in-law, Wajeeh Nuseibeh, who in turn invited me to come interview him in Jerusalem. To all of my interviewees and those who helped set up those interviews, thank you.

The good folks at Westminster John Knox were kind enough to offer me the opportunity to write this book, my second with them, before my first book, *Neighbor*, had sold a single copy. I am grateful for their faith and confidence, and I am thankful that they provided me the opportunity once more to work with Jana Riess, who is a fantastic editor. I owe a debt of gratitude to the whole team at Westminster John Knox, but especially to Jana.

My friends who work at and patronize Café do Canto in San José's Little Portugal have provided me with a good and stimulating place to write. Just before I finished this book, Joe, who worked behind the counter and who was particularly hospitable to me, returned unexpectedly to his home in Madeira. The Department of Homeland Security deported him after arresting him at work; I suspect their efforts seldom have yielded less security for the homeland than when they sent Joe packing. I pray life is kind to him, and I hope our paths cross again someday.

My parents' generosity helped support the travel and adventure that was a necessary part of writing this book. My children inspired me when I felt discouraged. I am grateful for the generations that are the bookends of my life. They keep my spine straight and help me to stand tall.

More than anything, I am more thankful than I can ever say for the beauty, intelligence, kindness, strength, and joy my wife, Anne Marie, brings to my life. Insofar as such virtues make their way into the words I write, they have their source in her.

INTRODUCTION

WHILE WRITING THIS BOOK I HAVE ATTEMPTED TO CAPTURE something of the spirit of my late aunt Donnabelle Mullenger, my mother's eldest sister, who was born in 1921 in the quintessential small town of Dennison, Iowa, and who, in a subtle but culturally significant way, stood up to and confronted America's irrational, Cold-War-era fear of communism.

After graduating from Dennison High School in 1938, my beautiful and talented aunt moved to Los Angeles, where she lived with my great-aunt Mildred and studied at Los Angeles City College. During her second year of studies she was crowned Campus Queen, her picture appeared in the *Los Angeles Times*, and all the right people noticed her. Before long she signed a contract with MGM. That contract and her subsequent work at MGM made her a star, but at the cost of her name. Mullenger sounded too German; Donnabelle sounded too much like the name of someone from a small town in western Iowa—which, of course, she was. Without consulting her, the studio bosses gave her a new identity: my aunt Donnabelle would, for the rest of her life, be known to the world as Donna Reed.

Aunt Donna had a successful career in film. In an era when the worth of a female actor was often measured by the men with whom she was cast, Aunt Donna starred opposite some of Hollywood's biggest leading men, including John Wayne, Rock Hudson, Mickey Rooney, Steve Allen, and most famously, Jimmy Stewart in the iconic holiday film *It's a Wonderful Life*. As Frank Sinatra's love interest in *From Here to Eternity*, she played a woman of ill repute and won an Academy Award.

Her greatest success, however, was not in film but on television as the star and uncredited coproducer of *The Donna Reed Show*. Officially, the producer of *The Donna Reed Show* was Tony Owen, who at the time was also Aunt Donna's husband. It was a joint effort, however, with Tony working the business end of production while Donna was in charge of everything creative and artistic. This is how my aunt was able—quietly, but with a strong maternal vibe—to reject America's fear of communism and stand up to the nation's most powerful purveyors of that fear.

During the 1950s Hollywood was a hard place to be if your politics happened to lean to the left. Anticommunist fervor swept the nation in the wake of World War II, and in what amounted to government-sponsored witch hunts, both houses of Congress conducted investigations and held hearings in an attempt to ferret out communists and their sympathizers, particularly those holding government jobs and those in positions to influence American culture through entertainment and the arts. During this time, which often is called the McCarthy era (so named for Senator Joseph McCarthy, a leader in the anticommunist movement), those in Hollywood who were deemed communist or communist-leaning were blacklisted, unable to work in film or television.

In 1960 my Aunt Donna helped bring the McCarthy era to an end by hiring blacklisted writers to work on *The Donna Reed Show*. It was a bold move. Not only was she risking her career, but she also was allowing suspected communists—the people Americans feared most—to write scripts for a television show that, for better or for worse, would shape, for generations, American ideas about what motherhood and family life should look like. She did not just give jobs to a few (real or suspected, current or former) communists; my Aunt Donna essentially invited the communists into the living rooms of millions of Americans each week for more than a decade. America survived. So did motherhood and the family. As far as I know, *The Donna Reed Show* inspired exactly no one to join the Communist Party. My aunt's instincts were vindicated: Americans really didn't need to be so afraid.[1]

LATTER-DAY MCCARTHYISM

There are significant analogues between the American fear of communism during the McCarthy era and the American fear of Islam at the beginning of the twenty-first century. The fear of communism and the fear of Islam are similar in that Americans have understood both to pose an existential threat to the United States. Congressional committees have held hearings to scrutinize both communists and Muslims, and Americans have been willing to abdicate civil liberties in the fight against the perceived threats of both communism and Islam.

Nowhere is the general American fear of Islam brought into clearer focus than in presidential politics since the ascendance of Barack Hussein Obama. Google "Muslim" and "Barack Hussein Obama," for example, and you will find a long list of Web sites that, with equal measures of alarm and certitude, proclaim that the forty-fourth president of the United States is a Muslim. It doesn't really matter that Barack Obama self-identifies as a Christian. Nor does it matter that even if Mr. Obama were a Muslim, nothing in the United States Constitution would prevent him from serving in the nation's highest office. The president, according to these Web sites, is a Muslim because he has Muslim relatives and a Muslim-sounding name; therefore he is a threat to America.[2]

As the 2012 presidential election heated up, a general fear of Islam showed no signs of abating. On June 13, 2011, at a debate for Republican presidential hopefuls, candidates addressed the question of whether or not Muslims are fit to hold cabinet-level positions in the executive branch. Republican contender and former Godfather's Pizza CEO Herman Cain, to enthusiastic applause, responded by saying he would have to think long and hard about appointing a Muslim to a position in his administration. "I would not be comfortable because you have peaceful Muslims and then you have militant Muslims—those that are trying to kill us." He went on to sound an alarm about Muslim law, sharia, being adjudicated in American courtrooms. "I don't believe in sharia law in American courts," Cain said. "I believe in American laws in American courts, period. There have been instances in New Jersey, for example, and there was an instance in Oklahoma, where Muslims did try to influence court decisions with sharia law. I was simply saying, very emphatically, American laws in American courts."[3]

Mitt Romney, the former Massachusetts governor and eventual Republican nominee, who as a Mormon is affiliated with an oft-maligned and usually misunderstood religious tradition, responded reassuringly, "Of course, we're not going to have sharia law applied in U.S. courts. That's never going to happen. We have a constitution, and we follow the law." He went on to sound a note of inclusion: "We recognize that people of all faiths are welcome in this country. Our nation was founded on a principle of religious tolerance. That's in fact why some of the earliest patriots came to this country and why we treat people with respect, regardless of their religious persuasion."[4]

It was a short-lived moment of goodwill. Former Speaker of the House Newt Gingrich, another aspirant vying for the Republican nomination, was quick to restore and exacerbate the paranoia inherent in Herman Cain's initial response. "Now, I just want to go out on a limb here," Gingrich said. "I'm in favor of saying to people, 'If you're not prepared to be loyal to the United States, you will not serve in my administration, period.' We did this in dealing with the Nazis, and we did this in dealing with the Communists, and it was controversial both times, and both times we discovered, after a while, there are some genuinely bad people who would like to infiltrate our country. And we have got to have the guts to stand up and say no." Gingrich's comments on Islam were among the most enthusiastically-applauded responses during the debate.[5]

CONFRONTING POPULAR MISCONCEPTIONS

If we were to ask Mr. Cain or Mr. Gingrich why they fear Muslims, the two men might respond that Islam is "a religion of violence." At first blush that answer, however ill-informed, might seem plausible. After all, in the twenty years preceding the publication of this book, militant Muslims committed some heinous acts of terrorism. Upon further examination, however, the idea that all Muslims should be feared because Islam is violent is flawed logic. While it is true that violence is, at times, perpetrated in the name of Islam, non-Muslims are violent and engage in acts of terrorism as well, yet the world's non-Muslim majority is not equally offended when non-Muslims are violent. For example, when Roman Catholics plant pipe bombs in Ireland, or evangelical Protestants murder abortion providers and destroy their clinics, Christianity does not become the focus of our fear. When Jewish settlers in the West Bank attack their Palestinian neighbors, building on their land and uprooting their olive groves, we don't fear that Jewish violence will spread beyond the Holy Land. We don't fear all Hindus for the militant extremism practiced by a radicalized few, nor do the repressions of Buddhist governments in Sri Lanka and Myanmar invoke widespread fear of Buddhism.

We do, however, fear Islam. I think the first and most important reason for our fear is archetypal. As I did research for this book, I discovered that non-Muslims—particularly European non-Muslims and their progeny in the New World—have been afraid of Muslims for centuries. The fear probably is rooted in the threat Europeans felt as the empire of the Muslim caliphs began to creep north and west into Europe from the seventh century to the eleventh, and certainly the European fear of Islam both inspired and was reaffirmed by the Crusades, the so-called reconquest[6] of Spain, and later European conflicts with the Ottoman Empire. For Americans, fear of and conflict with Islam and Muslims is almost exactly as old as our country itself. The United States' first war after gaining freedom from England was against Muslim pirates from North Africa and the states who sponsored their acts of terror, and our fear of Islam has never really departed from us.

Since the fall of communism and the First Gulf War, and especially since the terrorist attacks of September 11, 2001, writers and bloggers such as Pamela Geller, Daniel Pipes, Robert Spencer, Steven Emerson, Michelle Malkin, and David Horowitz—to say nothing of media personalities such as Glenn Beck and Rush Limbaugh—have discovered that there is good money to be made and lots of attention to be grabbed in the fear-purveying industry. Bowing to Mammon, they have stoked this historic and inchoate fear of Islam through demagoguery in the public square, and the results have been tragic.

On July 22, 2011, the day I finished writing the first draft of the manuscript for this book, a Norwegian man by the name of Anders Behring Breivik, after killing eight people with a bomb planted in downtown Oslo, attacked and murdered sixty-nine people attending a youth camp affiliated with Norway's left-leaning Labor Party. Before carrying out his attacks, Breivik wrote a tome of considerable length that credited Robert Spencer as an inspiration for his rampage.[7] Breivik also had a fondness for Daniel Pipes,[8] Pamela Geller,[9] and many of the other promoters of Islamophobia I have written about in this book. Such writers and thinkers claim to offer a cure for the encroachment of Islam into Europe and North America. It is a treatment for a nonexistent ailment; it is medicine that kills.

THE ILLUSION OF BALANCE

"But aren't you going to write about Muslim terrorists, anti-Semites, and woman-haters so that your book will be balanced?" Over the course of this project, friends and acquaintances who are disappointed to hear that I am writing a book that is Islam-friendly have asked me this question with a regularity that I found surprising and a little bit disturbing.

The short answer to the question is "no." I'm inclined to say that I'm not particularly interested in balance. I have an agenda. I want to soothe the anxieties and calm the fears around Islam that afflict so many of my non-Muslim friends and neighbors. But a more reflective response to the issue of balance must ask if an in-depth exploration of Islamic terrorism alongside an equal measure of ink dedicated to descriptions of peaceable and neighborly Muslims would, in fact, be balanced. It is a question of fulcrums. Despite the considerable havoc violent extremists have wreaked in the name of Islam, the number of such extremists is negligible in comparison to the population of Muslims worldwide. In order to create a "balance" between extremists and the rest of Islam, the fulcrum must be moved ridiculously far to one side. Such attempts at "balance" serve to distort rather than to clarify our understanding of Islam.

What I can say is that the following chapters present a balanced portrayal of Islam as I have encountered it in the Muslims I know. More important, I have endeavored to write this book honestly—to say what is true. My desire is to be judged on my attempts at truth-telling rather than by elusive standards of balance. It is clear to me that America needs more Donna Reeds, wise individuals willing to risk their reputations to calm our fears relative to Islam and its adherents. Unlike my famous aunt, I don't have a television show that can be used in the effort to overcome fear. I do, however, have a pulpit. I am a pastor who wants Christians everywhere to remember the words of Jesus, who promised us that when we know the truth, the truth will set us free.[10] My prayer is that the search for truth presented in these pages will bring freedom to those in bondage to a fear of Islam.

This book, written in the family tradition of confronting fear, is dedicated to my children, and I offer it to you in the hope that the people you meet in these pages, and the presentation of Islam you encounter in these chapters, will alleviate any fear that afflicts you and creates enmity between you and your Muslim neighbors, friends, and family members.

Part 1

The Keys to the Kingdom

Basics: What Is Islam?

It seems logical that a book on Islam for a non-Muslim audience should begin with some basic information that takes no prior knowledge of Islam for granted, and the most basic information involves the definition of terms. Each of the five main sections of this book begins with a "basics" interlude that addresses one of the key questions about the religion of Islam.

Islam—an Arabic word that derives from a root that can mean "peace" or "submission"—is a religion that is monotheistic (affirming a belief in one God) and Abrahamic (understanding that one God to be the same God worshiped by Jews and Christians). A Muslim is someone who practices Islam; the word "Muslim" is derived from the same root as "Islam" and means "one who submits" or "one who makes peace."

Muslims believe that the angel Gabriel appeared outside the city of Mecca to a prophet named Muhammad in the seventh century of the Common Era and, over the course of several years, revealed to Muhammad a new way of knowing and serving God. Muhammad memorized the words of the angel and repeated them to his friends, who transcribed them, preserving them for future generations in the form of Islam's holy book, the Qur'an.[1] "Qur'an" means "recitation."

In addition to the Qur'an, which is the most important source of religious inspiration for Muslims (see "Basics: What Is the Qur'an?" in part 4 of this book), Islamic faith and practice are also formed by the traditions (hadith, in Arabic) that remember the life and sayings of the Prophet. One such tradition records a conversation between Muhammad and the angel Gabriel, in which the Prophet and the heavenly being enumerate Islam's core doctrines:

- A belief in one God. This is probably the most important of Muslim beliefs: rigid monotheism distinguishes Islam from Christian Trinitarian beliefs about God and from the polytheism practiced on the Arabian Peninsula before the emergence of Islam.
- A belief in the angels of God (this belief is necessary for a religion whose holy book was revealed by an angel).
- A respect for other holy books of Western religions. Muslims believe the Qur'an is unique in its revelation of God, but they also honor the Jewish and Christian Bibles.

- A belief in the prophets of God. Muslims view Muhammad as the last and greatest of the prophets, but they also revere the prophets of the Jewish and Christian traditions, including Jesus, whom Muslims hold in high esteem.
- A belief in the judgment day and in the afterlife.
- A belief in divine sovereignty.[2]

Of course, Islam is much more than a simple list of affirmations, just as Christian belief is much more than what is contained in the Nicene Creed. Although that creed is affirmed by all Christians, it does nothing to explain Byzantine architecture, John Calvin's views on predestination, or the Pope's red shoes.

As with Christianity, in Islam there are various divisions, traditions, denominations, and schools of thought. While the two largest divisions of Islam—the Shiite and Sunni branches of the faith—date back to conflicts that occurred during Islam's earliest years (see chap. 5), other traditions, denominations, and schools of thought have arisen in the various historical, cultural, political, and social contexts in which Muslims have lived.

Chapter 1

THE CITY OF GOD

Glorious things of thee are spoken,
Zion, city of our God;
He whose word cannot be broken
Formed thee for his blessed abode.

John Newton[1]

JERUSALEM. AL-QUDS. THE NAVEL OF THE WORLD. THE VERY footstool of God. I arrived in this holy city through the well-ordered, rush-hour gridlock of the Jewish neighborhoods that lie to the west of what certainly must be the world's most beloved and disputed bit of real estate. As my journey continued, Western-style commuting gave way to chaotic third-world traffic patterns in the Arab neighborhoods in the eastern part of the city, where I found my hotel on the Mount of Olives.

It was dark when I arrived. I ate a meal of lamb kebabs accompanied by pita bread with seven different dips and fell asleep to the pulsating dance music of an Arab wedding. I was a long way from my home in northern California.

In the morning I looked out my window and found myself at the hub of Abrahamic spirituality, the intersection of the religious traditions whose followers the Muslims call "People of the Book." My hotel was perched atop the Mount of Olives, just up the hill from the Garden of Gethsemane, and just down the street from a Jewish settlement. My window looked directly over an olive grove that separates the hotel from a Carmelite convent. Across the street was an ancient Jewish cemetery.

As the sun rose over the monastery steeple, it gave the Crusader-built walls of Jerusalem's Old City a rosy hue, which faded to grey as the sun climbed higher, dispersing the shadows that covered the Kidron Valley and the cemetery established by the great Muslim leader Saladin. Three religions tell me that if the world had come to an end during my stay, I would have a front-row seat from which to witness the apocalypse. That is why so many people—Jews, Muslims, and a few Christians (most notably, according to tradition, the Blessed Virgin herself)—are buried nearby: when God returns to collect his own from among the faithfully departed, it's good to be first in line.

Bells rang, announcing prime. Young men from the nearby settlement walked past the hotel on their way to pray among the tombs of their ancestors, facing the Temple Mount, which is called Haram al-Sharif (or, the Noble Sanctuary) by those who have controlled it since the end of the Crusades (and for several centuries before the Crusades as well). The Temple Mount is an outcropping of rock that once was home to the Jewish temple, and some say will be again in the fullness of time. There, according to Jewish and

Christian tradition, Abraham made his aborted attempt to sacrifice Isaac, and there, a generation later, Jacob had his nocturnal vision of angels climbing the stairway to heaven.

Today the former Temple Mount is graced with the Dome of the Rock and al-Aqsa Mosque. After the cities of Mecca and Medina, it is Islam's third-holiest site. The Prophet Muhammad is said to have visited it, traveling on the wings of a celestial being. According to tradition, from there he ascended into heaven and, for a time, enjoyed the fellowship of the great prophets of old before returning to Mecca.

I traveled to Jerusalem because I wanted to test a hypothesis. In the years that followed the terrorist attacks of September 11, 2001—an epoch of wars and rumors of wars—I became sensitive to an oft-repeated narrative whose plot suggests an inescapable showdown between Christianity and Islam, an unavoidable conflict predicated on the fundamental incompatibility of two of the world's largest religions.[2] Such a pessimistic assessment of the religious landscape seemed like an exaggeration to me. In my opinion there was no reason Muslims and Christians should not be able to exist side by side in peace. To see if my optimism had merit, I went to the place on earth where Islam and Christianity have had the longest ongoing relationship.

In Jerusalem, Christians and Muslims haven't always enjoyed a peaceful coexistence—in fact, Christian attempts to expel Muslims from Jerusalem during the Middle Ages remain among the bloodiest examples of religious violence the world has ever known—but today Christians and Muslims live together in Jerusalem in relative peace. This truth is embodied in the person of Wajeeh Nuseibeh, the man who holds the keys—both symbolically and actually—to the peace enjoyed between Christians and Muslims in Jerusalem.

According to his business card, Mr. Nuseibeh is the "Custodian and Door-Keeper of the Church of the Holy Sepulchre."[3] It's a job that has been passed down in his family, from father to son, since the end of the Third Crusade; Nuseibeh family tradition says that the family had a similar position before the Crusades as well, since the days when Sheikh Umar (ca. 586–644), a companion and father-in-law of the Prophet and the second Muslim caliph, peacefully wrested control of Jerusalem from the Zoroastrian Persians. Umar respected the right of Christians to keep the churches in Jerusalem, including the Church of the Holy Sepulchre, which houses the traditional sites of Jesus' crucifixion and resurrection.

In the West, where conflict between Islam and Christianity all too often is considered to be the natural order of things, it is not well known that a Muslim family has, each day for centuries, opened and shut the great doors to the church that commemorates the place of Jesus' death and resurrection. Nor is it commonly known that this same family has used its role as custodians of Christianity's most sacred building to make peace and preserve the holiness of the place. But the relationship between the Nuseibeh family and the scene for the Easter story should be learned and remembered because it suggests that a better and more peaceable model for coexistence is possible. In fact, it has been fully operational for centuries in the city where Christianity and Islam have their most intimate interaction.

GETTING LOST

Now, if you're me, and if you're staying in a hotel on the Mount of Olives, east of Jerusalem's Old City, this is how you get to the Church of the Holy Sepulchre: you get lost. You head down the Mount of Olives on foot, whistling the hymn "All Glory, Laud and Honor" because this is the same route Jesus took in the procession Christians celebrate on Palm Sunday. You walk through Jewish cemeteries and past the little church that sits upon the ancient site commemorating the verse in Luke (19:41) where Jesus weeps over Jerusalem.

After passing through the Garden of Gethsemane, you come to a busy street, which you cross, risking your life, in the middle of traffic. You figure any gate into the Old City will do, since you don't know where you're going anyway, so you head in through the Lions' Gate and find yourself in a place for which there can be no preparation: it is a warren of streets, some of them made out of stairs, some not much larger than a hallway in a suburban home, none laid out according to a plan that makes sense to someone like you. It's morning, and the vendors are opening their shops, which further complicates matters because the streets are changing before your eyes as merchants set out everything from religious trinkets to hookahs, from incense to orange juice. It is an unfolding, blossoming place, filled with strange and wonderful colors and scents and sounds. You are not in Kansas anymore. In fact, you have no idea *where* you are.

From time to time you see markers that denote stations of the cross, so you figure you must be on the Via Dolorosa, the route walked by Jesus as he carried his cross from Pilate's house to Calvary, and you know that you are *going* to Calvary, so you cannot be too lost. But then you cannot find the next station, and someone wants you to come in his shop to buy a piece of pottery upon which are written the words "Shalom Y'all." "For you, very cheap, my friend," he tells you, but you blow him off because you've lost track of the Via Dolorosa, and you're starting to panic, just a little bit.

You see signs with arrows pointing to the Church of the Holy Sepulchre, but they lead nowhere. You realize that you're starting to go in circles because you keep running into the same guy selling pottery, and he keeps hoping you've changed your mind. By now you know he calls himself Mike and has a sister in Toronto. About the time you're getting desperate (and you're thinking of buying something from Mike just so he'll give you directions), you see a sign that reads "St. Helena Road," and you think to yourself, "What the hell." You know that Saint Helena, the mother of the emperor Constantine, was responsible for identifying most of the Christian holy sites in the place we now call Israel/Palestine, including your destination.

It turns out that St. Helena Road is a good bet. It's only about six feet wide and fifty feet long. It takes a dogleg turn at the gate to the Sheikh Omar Mosque, and you know you must be close because this has to be the same Sheikh Umar (you say Umar, I say Omar), the companion, father-in-law, and second successor of the Prophet, who first entrusted the Nuseibeh family with their custodial duties at the Church of the Holy Sepulchre. Saint Helena Road ends at a doorway through which you can glimpse a plaza. Once on the plaza, you turn to the left, and now finally you can see the facade of the church. The building itself is enormous—one of the largest structures in Old Jerusalem—but you'd never know it, because everything here is packed together so closely.

You're on time but not by much, and Mr. Nuseibeh is waiting for you, sitting on a pew just inside the doors he and his ancestors have opened each morning and closed each night for centuries.

That's how you get from the Mount of Olives to the Church of the Holy Sepulchre, at least if you're me.

WAJEEH NUSEIBEH

After welcoming me to the church, Wajeeh Nuseibeh invited me to sit down in what he called the "Muslim part of the church," which consisted of his pew and a narthex-like area that was probably six feet deep and twelve feet long. Along the wall were cupboards, from which he collected the key to the church, and proceeded to give me a demonstration of how the massive doors are locked each night and opened each morning.

Mr. Nuseibeh is a short man with a round face and a sturdy frame. His face is adorned with a well-trimmed moustache perched above an easygoing smile. He chatted in heavily accented English as he gave me an insider's tour of the building, which is divided between the Greek Orthodox Church, the Armenian Orthodox Church, and the Franciscan Order of the Roman Catholic Church. "Every stone is assigned to someone," my host told me,[4] "and some stones are divided. It's how we keep peace between the groups." Somehow, thrown into the mix, the Ethiopian Orthodox Church also has established itself as a claimant to the sacred space. They've built a monastery on the roof of the church and chapels along the staircase that leads from the roof to the ground. Inside the church they've placed an altar on the back of the structure—a church within a church, really—that covers what is believed to be Jesus' tomb.

It's hard to keep things straight. Mr. Nuseibeh told me, "Sometimes there are problems, arguments over who gets to clean the church, who gets to say mass, who gets to have a procession, so I make a schedule, and everyone must follow my schedule. This is why it is important that I am a Muslim. I am seen as being neutral."

To say that the Church of the Holy Sepulchre needs the Nuseibeh family is something of an understatement. At various times throughout history, the church's several claimants have decided not to abide by the Nuseibeh family's directions: the results have been absurd and, at times, tragic. On the front of the church a ladder rests on a ledge above the front door, and it leads to an upper window. Mr. Nuseibeh told me it was left as a monument to the time when, after an internecine dustup over some long-forgotten triviality, using a ladder and entering through the upper window was the only way the Franciscans could gain access to the sanctuary. This was in the year 1853. In 1808, the building was gutted by a fire that started as the result of a brawl between clergymen from different traditions arguing over rights to the church's spiritual treasures. When I visited, 202 years later, an alcove belonging to the Greek Orthodox Church but on loan to the Syrian Orthodox Church remained a burned-out ruin because no one had yet agreed on who got to restore the space, which happened to be the entrance to what's believed to be the Arimathea family tomb (that's Arimathea, as in "Joseph of"—he's the benefactor who placed Jesus in the tomb). In the Holy Land, where there's a shrine to everything, it's odd that the grave of so important a Christian saint is a charred hole in the wall of a fire-gutted chapel.

As Mr. Nuseibeh gave me a tour of the church, he took me to all of the building's holy sites and, in the Franciscan vestry, showed me the sword and spurs that once belonged to Godfrey, Duke of Bouillon (ca. 1060–1100), a leader in the First Crusade. After conquering Jerusalem, Godfrey held the title of Advocate of the Holy Sepulchre, which made him the de facto king of Jerusalem. (Not wanting to wear a golden crown in a city where Jesus wore a crown of thorns, Godfrey rejected a royal title; he did not, however, reject the power or wealth that came with the title.)[5]

The weapons of a crusading duke are not the only relics of the church's connection to holy war. In the stairway leading down to a chapel commemorating St. Helena's discovery of the true cross, Mr. Nuseibeh showed me hundreds of small crosses carved by Crusaders into the stone walls, yet for the Muslim custodian of its doors, the Church of the Holy Sepulchre is a sacred space.

As we sat together and talked on his bench by the great doors, Mr. Nuseibeh greeted priests, monks, and tour guides he considers to be his friends. Part of his job is to make sure that no one enters the church wearing shorts and that décolletage (plunging necklines were in that year) was covered. From time to time he scolded me for crossing my legs. We were sitting directly across from Calvary, after all, and like his Muslim forebears since the time of Sheikh Umar, it is Wajeeh Nuseibeh's job—his personal jihad, or struggle—to keep this Christian place holy.

He is proud of the work he does, proud to be part of a living tradition. "It's like being a king," he told me. He was describing the hereditary nature of his life's work, but "royal" seemed also to describe the pride he felt in his position.

COFFEE WITH CARDAMOM

It is a requirement of Wajeeh Nuseibeh's position that he press a lot of flesh, and because he could not give me his full and undivided attention there in the doorway across from Calvary, he invited me to his house later that evening. It is a comfortable, if somewhat formal, home located just outside the city wall. The house is large by the standards of this part of the city: it has a driveway and a small front yard. When I arrived, my host ushered me in and gave me coffee, apologizing for the fact that his wife was visiting family in Jordan. Evidently, in his universe, coffee made by a man is inferior, but I was more than satisfied. This was Arabic coffee, mixed with cardamom and sugar—truly a delight.

Before making my trip to Jerusalem, while researching the Nuseibeh family, I found conflicting information about the length of the special relationship between this particular family and the Church of the Holy Sepulchre, so I asked Wajeeh Nuseibeh to set the record straight. He told me that his family had arrived in the seventh century from Medina in Saudi Arabia, where they were early followers and companions of the Prophet. "We were among the first people in Medina to accept Islam," he explained. "We protected the Prophet, and we broke bread with him. One of our matriarchs was called 'One who receives him,' and with her husband and children she fed the Prophet and she protected him from the *kofar*, the unbelievers."

One of the faithful matriarch's sons—Mr. Nuseibeh's ancestor—accompanied Caliph Umar on his campaigns of conquest in territory once held by the Persian Empire (see chap. 5). These adventures of annexation brought Umar's armies to Jerusalem in 638, where they were welcomed by the Christian patriarch, who invited the conquering caliph to pray in the Church of the Holy Sepulchre. Umar declined the invitation, choosing instead to pray at a rock just across from the church. The patriarch was surprised—and perhaps a bit offended—but Umar was firm in his decision, knowing that if he prayed in the Christian church, his followers would do likewise, and eventually the church would become a mosque.

In gratitude for Umar's wisdom and sensitivity, the patriarch presented the caliph with the keys to the church, which Umar passed on to Wajeeh Nuseibeh's ancestor. The keys were kept in the family, passed from father to son, until 1099, when Crusaders took the city of Jerusalem. When the Crusaders conquered Jerusalem, the invading soldiers of Christ killed tens of thousands of Muslims, Jews, and Orthodox Christians, but a remnant of the Nuseibeh family survived by escaping to Nablus, where they remained until the sultan Saladin took Jerusalem from the Crusaders in 1187. Saladin restored the Church of the Holy Sepulchre to the Orthodox Church, and he gave the keys to the church back to the Nuseibeh family, in whose hands they remained until three hundred years ago, when the Ottoman Turks recruited a second family—the Joudeh family—to help in the work of guarding the keys.

For three centuries now, a member of the Joudeh family has conveyed the keys to a member of the Nuseibeh family, who has unlocked the church's massive doors and kept watch over the church during the day. Every night a Nuseibeh locks the doors and gives the keys back to a Joudeh. This arrangement is reaffirmed ceremonially three times during Holy Week each year. On Maundy Thursday the two key-keeping families formally present the keys to the leaders of the Franciscan Order. They do the same for the Greek Orthodox Church on Good Friday, and once again for the Armenian Orthodox leaders before their celebration of the

Easter vigil. At each ceremonial presentation, the keys are returned to the safekeeping of their Muslim custodians.

"They need us to be there because we know everything about the agreements that govern the church," Wajeeh Nuseibeh told me. "We are the neutral party between all the churches. We are like the UN. And we try to be friendly with everybody, and we are, indeed, good friends. I visit them, they come to visit me, they invite me to celebrate holidays with them. We are not just working: we are living as a bridge of peace between Christianity and Islam."

Mr. Nuseibeh refreshed my coffee as the evening began slipping into night in the City of God, a place that is timeless in a way that makes it seem disconnected from the modern world. Certainly the arrangement by which the Nuseibeh family keeps peace at the Church of the Holy Sepulchre seems out of place in a modern world. I asked him if his job remains full-time work that can support a family. "No," he told me. "I used to work in electronics, but I was able to retire and take this job when my father passed away." He impressed upon me that his family does not perform this service for free; they receive a small stipend of about $150 a month. Mr. Nuseibeh is training his son to take up the family duty one day, but at the moment his son is more interested in completing his education and making a living as a hairdresser.

As we were finishing our coffee, Mr. Nuseibeh got up and rummaged around in another room. He came back with a box of mementos—gifts he had received from visiting dignitaries. He had met many of the world's influential political and religious leaders, and many of them brought him gifts. He's particularly fond of a watch that was a present from Russian leader Vladimir Putin. He told me about his experiences meeting both Barack Obama and John McCain.

Behind his chair was a framed photo of Mr. Nuseibeh shaking hands with Pope John Paul II.

"I always greet them as equals," he told me. "None of this kissing of rings or bowing. In God's eyes we are the same. We are all brothers."

Wajeeh Nuseibeh walked me to the front gate of his house and showed me the place where he used to have a roof over his front porch. The old roof had rotted, and he needed to replace it, but in Jerusalem, at the time of this writing, the city government seemed to be doing everything it could to prevent Arabs from building or even repairing homes.[6] To fix his porch, Mr. Nuseibeh was looking at spending upward of $20,000 and countless hours in court just to get the necessary permits. He seemed disinclined to spend the money. The house looked fine, and an orange tree was growing up and would provide shade soon enough. The unrepaired porch would stand as a reminder that not everyone in Jerusalem shares Wajeeh Nuseibeh's vision of a city in which people share sacred space by keeping peace one with the other.

We said our goodbyes, and I took my leave, walking along the wall of the Old City, past the Lions' Gate and then up the Mount of Olives. Nighttime was falling, and muezzins from a dozen minarets were calling faithful Muslims to prayer as I returned to my hotel, taking the same path that Jesus took when he was in Jerusalem and wanted to pray in Gethsemane.

TOURISTS IN THE CITY OF GOD

After eating dinner in my hotel's dining room, I walked out into the gardens behind the hotel. A warm breeze was blowing up off the Dead Sea. During the day the view from the hotel's backyard looks out over the Kidron Valley as it wends its way into the Judean desert. The view was spectacular, but it was bisected by the ugliness of a wall that snakes its way through the landscape, separating Israel proper from the West Bank and the people who live there.

I hesitate to write about politics both because several years will have elapsed between my visit to Jerusalem and the publication of this book. A lot can happen over the course of several years, and the political situation is serious and complex enough that it deserves more time and ink than can be rendered faithfully at the tail end of a chapter in a book such as this. In the Holy Land, however, politics are unavoidable because life is entirely infused with politics. So I will say just this: when I asked Wajeeh Nuseibeh how the Israeli policies of occupation affected his work, he told me about frequent attempts by the Israeli government to give the keys of the church to Christian patriarchs who claim ownership of the church, thereby ending the delicate, peaceful balance brokered by generations of Nuseibehs at Christianity's holiest shrine. He was quick to make sure that I understood these attempts in a broader political context, with a gentle critique of Israel's occupation of Palestinian territories and its subjugation of Arab populations within its borders. "This land is not for you or for me: it is for everybody. It is the land of God, and we are all tourists here. We should respect everyone and be friends."

These are wise words, and while I'm not naive about the deep conflicts that have marked Jerusalem's past and almost certainly will characterize its future, still I am glad to know that I, as a tourist in life, have as traveling companions people like Wajeeh Nuseibeh.

Besides being a holy site for Christians, the Church of the Holy Sepulchre was ground zero for the Crusades. Taking possession of Christianity's most important shrine was a motive for the wars waged by Western Christians against Islam in the Middle Ages. To this day, the Crusades elicit bitter memory among Muslims around the world, yet for centuries a Muslim family has kept peace between Christians at the place that inspired the Crusades, a place where marauding knights by the thousands scratched crosses into the disputed stones in an effort to gain heaven's favor, stones that once echoed with the jingle of armor stained by Muslim blood.

It is a remarkable example of compassion that a family of Muslims should, for well over a thousand years, devote their lives to keeping peace between Christians who—at least historically—may not deserve such kindness. It is a gift, a reminder that conflict between Muslims and Christians is not inevitable. Though commentators and prognosticators— secular and religious, Christian and Muslim—have suggested that an apocalyptic clash between Christianity and Islam is unavoidable, still the pacifying presence of the Nuseibeh family at the Church of the Holy Sepulchre bears witness to the hope that those who seek God along separate religious paths can keep peace not just with one another but also *for* one another.

This knowledge, when put into practice, may be the key to a peaceable future between Muslims and Christians. That was my theory, anyway, but I knew I'd have to test it in places farther removed from Jerusalem's holy ground. I'd need to see if the peace I saw on Zion's mountain could be found in Silicon Valley. For an answer to that question, I would need to go home.

Chapter 2

A MUSLIM PATRIOT ACTS

O beautiful for patriot dream
That sees beyond the years;
Thine alabaster cities gleam
Undimmed by human tears.
America! America!
God shed His grace on thee,
And crown thy good with brotherhood
From sea to shining sea.

Katherine Lee Bates[1]

DO YOU WANT TO MEMORIZE THE NINETY-NINE NAMES for God? There's an app for that. Do you want an app that allows you to "memorize the Qur'an, to study the tafseer [commentary on the Qur'an], practice the points of articulation of the Arabic letters, [and to] read and understand the root words of the Qur'an," all from the gentle glow of your iPhone or iPad? Then "myQuran" is just the app for you.[2] Both apps (and several others) are designed and produced by Salik Productions, a Silicon

Valley startup that caters to the needs of a devout, hip, tech-savvy, Muslim clientele.

One of the partners in Salik Productions is Tahir Anwar, who also happens to be the imam of the South Bay Islamic Association, a mosque in San José, California, that Imam Tahir's father helped to found in 1982. Tahir started working at the mosque in 2000, at the tender age of twenty-two, after eight years of study at a madrassa in his ancestral village in India's Gujarat State. He had been on the job a little more than a year when the terrorist attacks of September 11, 2001, changed his life. I wanted to talk to him about the work of an imam in the post-9/11 world, but first I asked him about his crossover into the high-tech industry.

"Fortunately or unfortunately, I'm very tech savvy," he told me. "I have a BlackBerry *and* an iPhone." He laughed in the self-deprecating way we denizens of this electronically connected era do when we realize that some portion of our lives has been given over to the gadgets we gather unto ourselves. To be sure, it is a laugh familiar to most residents of California's Silicon Valley, but Tahir's connection to the San Francisco Bay area is more than just technological. Tahir's family moved from London to San José when he was four. His embrace of baseball was quick: he became a passionate fan of the San Francisco Giants. For a moment we basked together in the happiness of remembering the 2010 World Series victory by that band of outcasts and misfits. "When the Giants won the World Series, I was over the moon," he said. "I'm still over the moon. My wife, who is from India, had never seen me like this, and she asked where all this energy was coming from, and I told her, 'This is history. You have no idea what this means to us.'"

NOT YOUR TYPICAL IMAM

I'm not entirely sure where Imam Tahir finds time for nine innings of distraction. Besides being an imam and an entrepreneur, he is on the faculty of Zaytuna College (see chap. 3), where he teaches Islamic law, and he is deeply involved in the life and well-being of his community, which sets him apart from many of his colleagues.

"I'm not your traditional imam," he told me. "I look very traditional"—he has a beard like the San Francisco Giants erstwhile closer Brian Wilson, only Amish style, without a mustache; his head is shaved to a buzz cut under a white skullcap, and on the day we met, he was wearing an ankle-length garment that, to an untrained eye, was something between a Nehru jacket and a nightshirt—"but unlike other imams you won't just see me at the mosque leading prayers. I grew up here. This is my community. I want to be involved. I was born in London, and I have strong ties to my ancestral village in India, but when I'm in England or in India, my friends, family members, and neighbors treat me like a foreigner, because San José is home. I belong here."

According to Tahir, traditional imams spend most of their time in the mosque, leading prayers, instructing children on how to read the Qur'an, and teaching spiritual formation classes for adults. Typically imams don't get directly involved in wider public life, but Tahir hasn't been able to stay *un*involved in the issues that affect the broader community.

In 2000, when he was fresh out of his training and just starting out, Tahir tried to be a traditional imam, but it didn't last. I suspect that community involvement would be part of Imam Tahir's life regardless of world history, but the events of September 11, 2011, changed his job description. Before 9/11 his focus was on his congregation; after 9/11 he was out in the community as much as possible. "I was getting out there, removing stereotypes, educating people, doing a lot of speaking," he told me. "I was the young imam without an accent, and it worked. Everyone loved it. It was fun."

True confession: I did not expect to hear an American Muslim spiritual leader tell me that 9/11 made his life fun. The Council on American-Islamic Relations (CAIR)—America's largest Muslim civil liberties and advocacy organization—has reported a steady, year-to-year increase in civil rights complaints filed by Muslims between 1996, when fewer than a hundred complaints were filed, and 2008, when CAIR fielded more than 2,700 complaints.[3] Eighteen percent of CAIR's 2008 caseload came from California.

And CAIR isn't the only organization that noticed an uptick in anti-Muslim bias. The *New York Times* reports that in 2009 the Federal Government's Equal Employment Opportunity Commission received 803 reports of workplace discrimination against Muslims, an increase of 20 percent over 2008 and 60 percent over 2007.[4] The Anti-Defamation League,[5] the American Civil Liberties Union,[6] the Southern Poverty Law Center,[7] Amnesty International,[8] and Human Rights Watch[9] all have expressed concern over mistreatment of American Muslims, and with good reason. The Pew Research Center for People and the Press reports that 28 percent of Muslims report being looked at with suspicion, 22 percent say they have been called offensive names, 21 percent have been singled out for airport security, and 13 percent report being singled out by other law enforcement agencies.[10]

I needed help understanding the imam's definition of fun.

"Really," he told me, "it's been fun—challenging, but fun, because I have had to explore my role, to expand beyond being at the mosque for prayers. I've had to learn a lot about my community, and at the same time I've had the opportunity to teach others about my religion and my culture and my way of life. I'm not proselytizing, mind you, just educating. After 9/11 there was a void that I could fill with my presence. Being out in the community seemed like the best way I could teach folks about Islam, so I got involved. I don't even remember how many boards and committees I have served on as the 'Muslim' representative."

FLYING WHILE MUSLIM

I first met Tahir in 2007, on precisely one such committee on which he served as a "Muslim representative": San José's Human Rights Commission. I was part of a consortium of religious leaders and peace activists making a petition to the commission, and at that meeting Tahir had a weary look about him. After we introduced ourselves to each other, he told me that he'd arrived at the meeting just hours after getting off a flight from Europe. As the plane was landing in San Francisco, someone noticed him praying and alerted the flight crew. For his airborne prayer, Tahir was detained by the Department of Homeland Security in San Francisco. That Tahir was returning from Germany, where he had traveled at the invitation of the U.S. State Department to help train U.S. embassy staff about Islam, didn't seem to matter. He was on an airplane, praying while Muslim, and that was enough to get him detained.

In the years since terrorists used airplanes to attack the United States on September 11, 2001, airline travel has been difficult for American Muslims. The thwarting of at least two subsequent attempts to use airplanes as weapons of terror—one involving explosives in a would-be terrorist's shoe and one involving explosive underpants—has only made matters worse. As mentioned above, 21 percent of American Muslims report being singled out in airports for extra scrutiny. If one assumes (as I suspect we must) that not all Muslims travel by air, then the chances that a random American Muslim traveler will be designated for extra scrutiny in an American airport is fairly high.

In some cases the treatment of Muslims has gone beyond enduring extra security. In 2006, for example, six imams were arrested at the airport in Minneapolis–St. Paul after fellow travelers reported them for engaging in suspicious behavior. Said behavior, it turns out, was praying at the gate before boarding the plane and, once on the plane, not sitting together.[11] In 2011 the pilot of an Atlantic Southeast Airlines flight from Memphis, Tennessee, to Charlotte, North Carolina, expelled two Muslim men off his airplane. Both men had been subjected to extra security—probably because of their use of traditional garb—and both had been cleared to fly. However, the pilot refused to operate the plane with the men aboard. It is fitting, perhaps, to note that the Muslim men—both academics—were on their way to attend a conference on anti-Muslim discrimination. As of this writing, a lawsuit is pending.[12]

Imam Tahir is no stranger to such treatment while flying. When I reminded him about our first meeting, his memory of it was vague because for Tahir, difficulty going through customs is always part of the travel experience. "In the last three years," he told me, "I've taken twelve trips overseas, and coming home, I've been stopped by homeland security twelve times." The last time he was delayed, he was with his twelve-year-old son, who suffered a severe reprimand from gun-toting customs enforcement agents for passing the time by playing on his dad's iPhone.

The experience was still a bit raw in Tahir's mind. He became animated. "I know for a fact," he said, "that I've served my community and I am more loyal to my city and to my government than that immigration officer, because for him it's probably a nine-to-five job, and I know how much I have put—in terms of hours and sweat—toward making my city a better place, whether it be planting trees or feeding homeless folks, or teaching members of my mosque and helping them to be loyal and productive citizens of the United States. As an imam, I can stand up on a Friday prayer service and I can say, 'Listen: I need a group of people who will go with me to East San José to cook lunch for three hundred people; and after we're done with that, we're going to go plant trees,' and I swear to God I have the power to round up a hundred people in no time. That officer doesn't have that power."

He was quiet for a moment and then relented. "It's a flawed system, and I've had good officers and I've had bad officers, and I'll defend the guy who yelled at my son because in my faith I'm commanded to make seventy excuses for everyone. So maybe he's had a bad day, maybe he lost a family member, maybe he didn't sleep the night before because his child was at the hospital—I don't know. But even after all of that, there are certain courtesies that must be extended, and when they are not extended, it's awful.

"If I ever write a book," he told me, "I will devote an entire chapter on my ordeals flying into the United States." Still, he didn't want to leave the topic of international travel on a down note, so he told me about a friend and fellow scholar who came from England for a visit. It took a lot of convincing on Tahir's part to get his friend to fly from London to San Francisco, but eventually Tahir prevailed, and the two traditionally dressed, long-bearded imams went for a California road trip. "I took him to LA, I took him to San Diego, I took him to Yosemite and Sequoia National Park, I took him to Tahoe, and at the end of the trip he's like, 'America *is* the place to be.'

"I asked him why he changed his mind, and he says, 'because in ten days we haven't met one person who has been rude to us or made fun of us. When we talk to people, they are friendly and kind.'" Tahir got a gleam of pride in his eyes. "This is California, and we were just two guys being tourists, eating at Denny's, staying in motels, and seeing the sights. In England you still find a bit of racism against brown people, but not here, so my friend was like, 'This is a great place!' And I said, 'Yes, it is.'"

AMERICAN MUSLIM OPTIMISM

Imam Tahir's optimism and patriotism surprised me, but they shouldn't have. What I didn't know, going into the interview, is that an overwhelming number of leaders in American mosques hold views similar to Tahir's, and that the United States has improved in the estimation of most American Muslim leaders in the years since 2001. For example, in a 2011 poll of Muslim religious leaders, 97 percent either "agree" or "strongly agree" when presented with the statement "Muslims should be involved in American society." Ninety-one percent either agreed or strongly agreed that Muslims should be involved in the political process. When the same questions were asked in 2000, the positive response was 2 percent lower. Despite the fact that a high percentage of Muslims perceive hostility from their fellow Americans, only 25 percent of Muslims leaders agree or strongly agree that the United States is hostile toward Islam. In 2000 a full 50 percent of Muslim leaders agreed that the United States is hostile toward Islam. In 2011, some 24 percent of mosque leaders believed that America is an immoral society, a number that had dropped from 56 percent in 2000.[13]

The pro-American optimism that permeates much of the American Muslim community and that is so evident in the life of Imam Tahir Anwar is both refreshing and contagious. It stands as a corrective to those who present Islam as an existential threat to American life; it is a reminder that true patriotism recognizes no sectarian bigotry.

As he walked me to the door of his office, I asked Tahir about the building that housed his mosque. It looked to me as if it might have been designed by the legendary California architect Julia Morgan. Tahir didn't know anything about the architect (probably not Julia Morgan, it turns out), but he did know that before becoming a mosque, the building belonged to the American Legion. This is remarkably apt because when I imagine American Legion halls, I think of places where American patriots gather and think together about how they might serve their communities. If Imam Tahir is in any way representative of the Muslims who come together for prayer at the South Bay Islamic Association mosque, then the former American Legion Hall in downtown San José, even if it has changed ownership, continues to serve such a function.

As I walked away from Tahir's mosque, my mind wandered back to Jerusalem and to the Church of the Holy

Sepulchre. I thought of Wajeeh Nuseibeh and about how, for centuries, a Muslim family has considered it a sacred duty to safeguard the holiness of Christianity's most important shrine, even though the church still bears the marks of the Crusaders, who slaughtered tens of thousands of Muslims during roughly two hundred years of holy war. It's not all that different from the ways in which Imam Tahir—and most other American Muslim leaders—work to preserve and promote the well-being of American society, even when much of America treats Muslims with suspicion.

Imam Tahir and Wajeeh Nuseibeh are cut from the same spiritual cloth, and it makes me happy that both men—and countless men and women like them—have been inspired by Islam to make the world a better place for all of God's children.

Part 2

Islam in the Capital
of the Birkenstock Nation

Basics: Who Is Allah?

"Allah" is the Arabic word for "God." The word "Allah" is a contraction that combines a definite article and the Arabic word for "deity,"[1] which means "Allah" could literally be translated as "the god." In common usage, however, Allah is a proper noun that refers to the God who is worshiped in the Abrahamic religious traditions (the Arabic definite article in "Allah" functions much in the same way that the capital "G" functions in English when "god" becomes "God").

Though Allah is the name for God most frequently associated with Islam and most commonly used by Muslims, it is a name that predates Muhammad and the rise of Islam. Muhammad understood himself to be a prophet in the

Abrahamic tradition. As such, he invited his followers to worship God as God is understood by Jews and Christians, and he directed his followers to speak of God as Allah, which was (and still is) the name Arabic-speaking Jews and Christians used for God.

Allah also was a name used by pagan Arabs in reference to the creator god who was worshiped at Mecca before the advent of Islam.[2] One reason Muhammad's message found such success in Arabia may have been because he did not ask pagans to give up their old beliefs entirely. His message was to be a corrective. It asked pagans to understand that the Allah they knew from generations of paganism was, in fact, the God of Abraham, long since hidden by syncretistic idolatry.[3]

In the Jewish and Christian traditions, God—or Allah, if you happen to speak Arabic—has many names, such as "The Holy One of Israel," "El Shaddai" (which means "God of the Mountain"), and "Father." Most of the biblical names for God describe God in some way. The same is true for Allah in Islam. In addition to Allah, Islamic tradition identifies ninety-nine names for God, all of which describe God, speaking of God's perfection, majesty, and beauty. While Muslims, like Jews, reject the Christian notion of the Trinity, none of the attributes of Allah that are affirmed by Muslims would seem unfamiliar to Christians.

Interestingly, the attributes and adjectives used as names for God in Islam are not all masculine. As God is transcendent, God has no gender. For Muslims, as for Christians and Jews, Allah is immortal, omnipotent, omniscient, and all-loving; and Allah would be unknowable, except that God has made God's self known to humanity. According to Islamic belief, this self-revelation is contained in the words of the Qur'an, through which humanity is invited into a spiritual life that is rooted in and nurtured by the love of God.

Chapter 3

IMAM ZAID SHAKIR AND THE EDUCATION OF AMERICAN MUSLIMS

The holy spirit
has revealed truth from your Lord
to stabilize those who believe.

Qur'an 16:102

ONCE A YEAR, IN THE ISLAMIC MONTH OF *DHU AL-HIJJAH*,[1] millions of devout Muslims descend upon the holy cities of Mecca and Medina for a pilgrimage known as the hajj, which commemorates and acts out the stories of Abraham, Ishmael, and Hagar's journey into the Arabian Peninsula. It is an ancient religious practice that predates Islam itself, and it is one of Islam's five pillars, a sacred duty: at least once in a lifetime all Muslims who are able are required to make the journey and to participate in the peregrinations of the hajj.

Each year, faithful Muslims who do not make the hajj gather for prayer and celebration on the last day of the pilgrimage. The holiday is called *Eid al-Adha*, or the festival of the sacrifice, a reference to Abraham's willingness to sacrifice his son, and to God's faithfulness in providing a ram to be sacrificed in place of the child.[2] During *Eid al-Adha*, Muslims are supposed to dispense charity, make peace with one another, and worship in their finest clothing.

The worship is an impressive experience, or at least it was for me when in 2010 I attended a gathering of Muslims affiliated with Imam Tahir's mosque. The old American Legion Hall downtown is too small to accommodate everyone who wanted to gather in prayer, so each year Tahir's mosque rents the Santa Clara County Fairgrounds, where they pray together in an exhibition barn that harkens back to the days when Silicon Valley was a place of orchards and dairies. The room is cavernous, an echo chamber without acoustical warmth. The floor is a cement slab—cold on the November morning when I attended the service, during which Muslim men and women walked without shoes on floor coverings that were about the thickness of a tarp.

In the room, the ductwork is huge—able to provide ample ventilation for humans and animals. Sparkling Mylar garlands and party lights added a bit of gaiety, but there was no getting around the fact that this was a temporary mosque, chosen for its ability to hold a cast of thousands and not because it was an architectural gem.

Shafath Syed, a young South Asian man who, like his father before him, is a layperson and the president of the South Bay Islamic Association, called the assembled group to order with a passionate plea for community involvement. "Our nation and our world are facing a variety of issues," he told the gathered crowd. "People are out of work, poverty is on the rise. We face a host of social, economic, and environmental issues that need to be addressed. We need to stand for justice, and we need to do our part to meet the needs of society. So get involved—it will fulfill you in ways that nothing else will."[3]

He went on to clarify that getting involved meant reaching out. He cited a statistic claiming that most non-Muslims in America have never knowingly met a Muslim. "We need to do our part to bridge the gap of misunderstanding," he said. "We need to meet non-Muslims. We need to invite them into our homes so that they can see that we're just like everyone else."

Next, a young scholar—a blond-haired, blue-eyed Midwesterner—addressed the crowd, giving a lecture on the meaning of the hajj. The talk had something to do with how keeping the pillars of Islam, including the hajj, helps us to live as God intended. That is a fine message, but a lot of it was in Arabic, and I confess that I was getting distracted by all the different kinds of hats worn by the gathered faithful. Muslim men—like their Jewish and Sikh counterparts—often cover their heads during prayer. It is not an absolute requirement, but many men do it, and the hats they choose are determined entirely by the cultures in which they were raised.

In a predominantly Muslim country such as Tunisia, most of the hats in a neighborhood mosque likely will be similar, but in San José—as in much of the United States, where members of a local mosque are likely to come from all over the Muslim world—the hats are a beautiful reminder of Islam's diversity. Without their hats, Muslims from Indonesia, Malaysia, and southern China might look alike to a Californian like me; but the hats set them apart and made the differences apparent, even as they joined together in prayer, their shoulders touching as first they stood, then bowed, then knelt, then prostrated themselves toward Mecca, where millions of their fellow Muslims were engaged in the ancient, sacred pilgrimage.

Some of the hats were brightly embroidered with silk thread, while some looked like they were crocheted using a doily pattern. I'm pretty sure that one of the doily hats had a Magen David—a star of David—pattern in its design. Some of the men wore turbans, others the round caps of Afghan tribesmen. One guy was wearing a golf cap backward. Some of the men sported the knit caps of urban hipsters, and one young man was dressed in a purple ski cap, with reflective aviator sunglasses, which looked like something Erik Estrada would have used on *CHiPs*, worn backward on his neck. A little boy was wearing a Where's Waldo? hat, only it was green. About half of the men present had no hats at all, which, as far as I can tell, is a reflection of American culture, where men take their hats off in church. I was hoping that the Americans would be represented by someone in a fine felt fedora—something that might be seen on William Powell in one of the *Thin Man* films—but really, America is all of the above. It is the bareheaded Californian and the hipster youth. America is Muslim immigrants from all over the world.

The faces under the caps were South Asian and Arab, African and from the Far East. A few of the faces belonged to folks of European descent—one of the men I met while celebrating *Eid al-Adha* was born in Finland, raised on Michigan's Upper Peninsula, and is married to a woman from Vietnam. This is an international faith, making its home in a country built by immigrants. It should be a perfect fit.

Imam Tahir's younger brother—who also happens to be an imam—led the gathered faithful in prayer. Tahir was on the hajj, but from Mecca he sent greetings to the congregation via text message: "Peace be with you" (or more likely, "Peace B w/ U"). As they prayed, standing, bowing, kneeling, and prostrating, holiness filled the cavernous room. The haunting sounds of Arabic echoed off the tin roof and peace—palpable holy peace—was with us indeed.

Of course, Islam in America is more than the sum of hats (or bare heads) in a temporary mosque at a fairground in the Silicon Valley. Islam in America is also about faithful living that affects the life of a community. For me, hearing the leader of a local community of Muslims call for Islamic involvement in the issues facing our nation, and for outreach to non-Muslims, was as encouraging as it was inspirational. It seemed to be an expression of a larger movement within Islam that seeks to influence American culture in a positive way, just as reform movements within Christianity have connected matters of faith with the needs of the world.

The calls for community involvement issued to the Californian Muslims gathered for *Eid al-Adha* prayers at the Santa Clara County Fairgrounds, with only minor alterations, could have been spoken at gatherings of Christians who were concerned about hunger, or social and economic justice, or peacemaking. I felt at home.

FINDING IMAM ZAID SHAKIR

My sense of connection at the *Eid al-Adha* prayer service mirrored a sense of comfort I felt while talking to Imam Zaid Shakir, a distinguished American Islamic scholar and one of the founding faculty members of Zaytuna College, the first four-year Muslim liberal arts college in the United States. Zaytuna—which means "olive" in Arabic[4] and was named after an important Tunisian center of Islamic thought—was about halfway through its first semester when I visited Imam Zaid Shakir. We met on the Zaytuna campus in Berkeley, California, just a block from People's Park, which is famous for its role as a gathering place for students and hippies during the halcyon days of Berkeley's psychedelically colorful past.

That I found Zaytuna College there just meters from one of the sixties-era countercultural chakras was a feat of considerable effort because I got lost in Berkeley while trying to find the place. I am not the first person to get lost in Berkeley (either geographically or spiritually), but I went astray under the direction of my iPhone, which I trust to guide me in such situations.

After my cell phone sent me to Zaytuna's old address, I ended up running about a mile and a half in penny loafers, past the excellent bookstores, world-class restaurants, and tie-dyed neohippiedom that is Berkeley in the twenty-first century until finally, ten minutes late for my interview, I found the college in the basement of a Baptist seminary. I walked into the foyer of the space the Muslims have rented from the Baptists, and to my right a group of about a dozen students were helping Imam Zaid unpack books for the college library. Those students represented pretty much the entire student body.

Imam Zaid greeted me warmly and led me into a classroom, where we sat at a conference table and talked about his hopes for the future of Zaytuna College. But first I asked him to tell me a little bit about himself and how he became one of America's most prominent Muslim leaders. As a Christian who is accustomed to hearing testimonies of conversion and redemption, the story Imam Zaid told me sounded familiar.

Imam Zaid was born in Berkeley and given the name Ricky Mitchell. He was the second of seven children, and at the time of his birth his father was serving in the United States Navy. After his father's discharge, the family moved first to Georgia—where Imam Zaid's mother had been born and raised—and eventually to a public housing project in New Britain, Connecticut.[5] He was raised in a fairly traditional black Baptist church but didn't really start thinking about spiritual matters until his senior year in high school when, while playing football, he suffered a shoulder injury that required surgery. "That got me thinking about the more serious things of life," he told me. "There had to be more to life than playing football or going to parties or the usual things that kids in high school do—well, for some it gets old real fast, and I was in that category, just going through the motions, going along to get along. But pretty soon you realize you're not being true to yourself or to your values."[6]

The young man who would grow up to be an important American Muslim leader started to ponder the meaning and purpose of life. He decided to examine spiritual matters, but before he looked to heaven, he examined the people in his neighborhood, at the various levels of vice going on in their lives and at the dead ends that seemed to await most of his contemporaries. "Seeing that, I was thinking, 'How could that be changed?' And that motivated me to start looking at religion."

Imam Zaid Shakir's experiences in the African American Baptist tradition provided him with the extent of his exposure to religion. He recognized this limited knowledge of spiritual matters to be something worth changing, so he began to study religion more seriously. He concluded, based on what he told me was "a superficial level of analysis," that the Bible was full of contradictions, and that the history of Christianity was too political and driven by human events to be rooted in divine origin.

This led to an aversion to religion. Zaid got involved in communism and became an atheist, but not for long. "I was thinking the communist revolution was how we were going to effect change, but eventually I realized that there were some serious flaws in the ways communists think," he explained.

A particular vexation among the creeds of communism was the concept of dialectical materialism, a belief that in the course of human history opposing forces (thesis and antithesis) resolve into a balance (synthesis).[7] As he thought about dialectical materialism, he found himself asking, "OK, where did the first thesis come from? If you have thesis, antithesis, [and] synthesis and this is how history proceeds, who produced the first thesis? Was it just 'poof' and it's here?"

In the end, these questions led to God. "I concluded there has to be a creator who originated everything, and there has to be something that gave life to the inorganic. There has to be a Life Giver, an Arranger, and Organizer, and that got me searching for God again." Through an interest in Eastern religious traditions, Zaid was briefly involved in Transcendental Meditation, but it didn't last. His fundamental religious inclinations were too rooted in a need for social transformation. "I was meditating and even becoming enlightened to a certain extent," he told me, "but I looked around myself and said, 'This isn't doing anything for anyone else. It's not doing anything to effect change. It's a selfish approach to religion.'"

Enter Islam. "Someone heard I was on this spiritual journey, and they gave me a book called *Islam in Focus.* When I read that, I said, 'This is it; my questions are answered. There's an individual program, a family program, and a societal program.' I knew some Muslims in my vicinity—I was actually in the air force at that time—so I went and became a Muslim."

A conversion to Islam begat a recommitment to learning. Before joining the air force, Imam Zaid had been a student at Central Connecticut University; upon his discharge from the air force, he finished his undergraduate degree at American University in Washington, D.C. There he majored in intercultural communication, and there, by cross-matriculating at Georgetown, he began his study of Arabic. His education continued with a master's degree from Rutgers and further studies in Arabic at the University of Cairo. "From the beginning," he told me, "most Muslims begin to study because Islam is a knowledge-based religion, and over time you study, and you realize you need to study more."

For a time, Imam Zaid Shakir's formal education was interrupted by teaching—he returned from Egypt to the States and taught political science as an adjunct professor at Southern Connecticut University—and by the work of starting and leading a mosque. But before long he returned to his studies, first in Damascus and later in Morocco, where he received formal training in Islam.

Imam Zaid finished his studies and returned to Connecticut in 2001; in 2003, he moved to California to work for what, at the time, was called Zaytuna Institute. "When Zaytuna was started, the vision was just to teach folks the basics of the religion, but as the work of Zaytuna went along, the need for accredited institutions of higher education became apparent."

ZAYTUNA COLLEGE

In 2008, after four years of planning, Zaytuna started a pilot program with just five students—to see what kind of curriculum could be used in an American Muslim college. The founders of Zaytuna—who included Imam Zaid Shakir, Hatem Bazian (see next chapter), and the world-renowned American scholar Shaykh Hamza Yusuf—wanted to develop a program that found a balance between Arabic language studies and Islamic sciences on the one hand, and Western-style humanities and social sciences on the other. Two years later, in 2010, Zaytuna College opened its doors with a student body of fifteen. The college has applied for accreditation with the Western Association of Schools and Colleges; the accreditation process takes four to seven years, and Zaytuna's faculty and administration anticipate a positive outcome to the process.

Zaytuna College is filling an important niche in American higher education. While Zaytuna—with its tiny student body—is the only Muslim college in the United States, Muslim primary and secondary education is better established. Currently, there are roughly forty thousand students enrolled in Muslim elementary and secondary schools in the United States,[8] and many of those students may want to earn an undergraduate degree from a Muslim college.

The potential for Zaytuna's growth is huge, as is interest in Arabic language training and Islamic studies programs at secular colleges and universities. At Duke University, for example, the number of students studying Arabic qua-drupled (from fifteen to sixty) between 2001 and 2006;[9] the University of Chicago reported a similar growth in Arabic language courses and a parallel increase in students inter-ested in Islamic and Middle Eastern studies in the years fol-lowing 2001.[10]

Clearly, the United States is ready for Zaytuna College, and Imam Zaid hopes the institution will help its students prepare for life in modern America by integrating a centuries-old faith into life in the twenty-first century. "We want to bring the text together with the context," he told me. "The Islamic studies [courses] and the Arabic language courses help to teach the religion with all of its nuance, and then the social science and humanities help to contextualize it in this twenty-first-century American environment that we find our-selves in. One without the other is insufficient."

His articulation of the purpose of an Islamic education actually sounded quite a bit like what I used to hear as a stu-dent at Westmont, a Christian liberal arts college in Santa Barbara, California, when, at the opening convocation of each academic year, the college president would address the student body and remind us of the purpose of a Christian liberal arts education. Like students at Zaytuna, we were supposed to let our faith inform our studies and our learn-ing inform our faith. Also, we were supposed to be molded by our faith and our learning so that as educated evangelical Christians, we could make an "impact" on the world.

I asked Imam Zaid if he hoped his students would, as educated Muslims, have an impact on American society. As he responded, he became very animated.

"Absolutely!"—here he popped up in his chair—"but in the natural course of things, not going out of their way to have a positive impact, which usually leads you nowhere, but in the natural projection of their lives. If they choose to study Islam further, if they choose to study law or medicine, or if they just end their studies at the bachelor level and be a housewife or a working man, they'll do whatever they end up doing in a way that impacts those their lives come into contact with. I like to think that that impact would have something to do with the education they have received here."

When I was a student at Westmont, the president also would express the hope that I and my fellow students would, as educated evangelicals, be an asset to the church. I asked Imam Zaid if he had similar expectations for the students at Zaytuna as active members of local Muslim communities.

He told me he did. "We hope, more than anything, that Zaytuna will work to standardize the understanding of Islam, because now we have Muslims from sixty or seventy different countries in America. Some of them have studied the religion, some of them haven't studied anything, some of them think that the cultural environment they grew up in *is* the religion. So that all comes here, and everyone is thrown together into a ring in which there is no referee, no one to say, 'Listen, that was a low blow; you cannot do that; listen, you have to stay in the ring; you cannot go out of the ring and pull someone out; the contest is in the ring.'

"We hope that Zaytuna College and the students that leave here can be that referee, which helps to establish order and helps to convey the stability that Islam historically has had. One of the problems contemporarily is that the rudder has been lost, so the ship is very much exposed to the vagaries of the sea. If the wind comes one way or the waves come another way, then the ship is buffeted, without a rudder to steer safely though the storm."

A mixed metaphor, but fair enough. I have no doubt that the existence of what Imam Zaid hopes to help establish in Berkeley—a fully accredited and vibrant Islamic university—would strike fear into the hearts of many Americans and provide ample fodder for the rhetorical canons of those who would have us regard Islam with trembling dread. But to me, Imam Zaid's vision for the nascent Zaytuna College sounded exactly like the vision I imagine must have been shared by the founders of my alma mater, or of any of the hundreds of American Christian colleges that are spread out across all fifty states. With an overabundance of Christian colleges in America, I'm sure we can make room for an Islamic college.

In parting, I asked Imam Zaid if there was anything else he wanted the Christian readers of this book to know. There was. He wanted my readers to understand that Muslims are not trying to take over America, and that 99 percent of Muslims are living peacefully in the United Sates, trying to make a living, trying to take care of their families, trying to take advantage of the benefits that are present in American society, trying to contribute in a positive way to the society.

"Some people think about Islam in apocalyptic terms, as if Islam and Christianity are engaged in some kind of cosmic endgame. These people are divorced from reality. They might be truly afraid that a handful of Muslims who can barely keep the lights on in the mosque are somehow going to take over a society as vast and complicated, as strong institutionally, as the United States, but such a belief is nonsense."

Imam Zaid is confident that his students at Zaytuna College will help to create an American future less marked by fear of Islam. "Zaytuna graduates will be educated," he told me. "That gives our students a real advantage. None of the leaders of the radical Islamic movements have any theological training. Bin Laden was in business; his right-hand man went to medical school and is a doctor. These people are autodidacts, and because they are self-taught, they can read the Qur'an, and they can even read it more deeply that someone who is formally trained, but they're not trained in the interpretive tools to understand the Qur'an in a rich and relevant way. And the people opposing them—people like Robert Spencer [see chap. 10]—they're in the same category. In terms of Islamic studies, they're autodidacts, and so both arrive at this very superficial understanding of Islam because they haven't studied the legal and interpretive tools, the rhetoric as it relates to the Arabic language, or exegesis. They look at the text superficially and arrive at their own conclusions, and use historical anomalies, in some cases, to justify those conclusions. That's not a healthy and productive way to approach religion."

He's right, of course. Ignorance is not a peaceable or productive way to approach religion—one's own or anyone else's. That is why I wrote this book, and why I found myself, among other places, at the Santa Clara County Fairgrounds observing the last day of the hajj with a group of strangers in nifty hats.

After the *Eid al-Adha* prayer service was over, I walked out of the fairgrounds' exhibition hall and into a glorious autumn day. The organizers of the event had hired a small carnival to entertain the kids, with four or five rides twirling happily screaming kids into the air. I suspect some of those children will grow into adulthood as students at Zaytuna College. If they are lucky enough to study under Imam Zaid, they will be in good hands. They are the face of Muslim America's future. With the wisdom of people like Imam Zaid Shakir, both Islam and America will thrive.

Chapter 4

A JIHAD GROWS
IN BERKELEY (OR NOT)

Now when someone says, "Hell no, we won't go,"
What they mean is "to Berkeley."

Roy Zimmerman[1]

THE CITY OF BERKELEY IS THE LEFT VENTRICLE OF NORTHERN
California's Liberal Bleeding Heartland, and it's a great
place to eat. I found a nice French restaurant down on
Shaddock Avenue, in a neighborhood that locals sometimes
call "Gourmet Gulch." The eatery sat a few blocks from
the famed Chez Panisse; and it wasn't quite Chez Panisse,
but the food was still tasty, and the establishment was brilliant with local color. We patrons were packed together like
les sardines. At the far end of the room, a group of African American academics was talking about the sociological

effects of urban renewal; next to me three women of my mother's age were discussing the literature of Joyce Carol Oates and speculating on what it would be like to have sex with Jerry Brown, the former and current governor of the Golden State. I was eating a bowl of cassoulet and drinking a glass of Chateauneuf-du-Pape.

My God, I love Berkeley!

I was in town to interview Professor Hatem Bazian, a lecturer in Arabic in the department of Middle Eastern Studies at the University of California, who is, according to a list compiled by conservative activist David Horowitz, one of the 101 most dangerous professors in America.[2]

I first met Dr. Bazian in the spring of 2002 when, during a national outpouring of interfaith goodwill that followed the tragic terrorist attacks of September 11, 2001, we co-taught an adult education class on the three major Abrahamic religious traditions. Joining us in teaching the class was a Conservative rabbi from Walnut Creek, California. It was a good class. As the representative of the faith in which the students had the least interest, I was privileged to watch as Hatem and the rabbi interacted in a friendly and mutually respectful dialogue even when the subject of Israel/Palestine came up. The rabbi was unapologetic in his support for Israel, and Hatem Bazian—who was born in Jordan to Palestinian refugees from Nablus in the West Bank—was steadfast in his desire to see justice for his people. The two men of faith engaged the delicate issues that divided them with respect, humor, and honesty. The experience left me feeling hopeful that real and productive dialogue around Israel and Palestine is a possibility.

Though we parted on friendly terms, for two years Professor Bazian's name seldom crossed my mind until I was surprised by an e-mail forwarded to me by a member of my church who was unaware of my prior association with Dr. Bazian. This e-mail alerted me to the threat of jihad in America at the hands of, among other people, Professor Hatem Bazian. The e-mail quoted Hatem's speech at a gathering of antiwar protestors in San Francisco on April 10, 2004: "We're sitting here and watching the world pass by, people being bombed, and it's about time that we have an Intifada in this country that changes fundamentally the political dynamics here."[3]

The other statement that has earned Hatem Bazian the ire of his detractors actually shows him quoting from the hadith, the collected sayings of the Prophet: "In the Hadith, the Day of Judgment will never happen until you fight the Jews. They are on the west side of the river, which is the Jordan River, and you're on the east side until the trees and stone will say, 'Oh Muslim, there is a Jew hiding behind me. Come and kill him!' And that's in the Hadith about this, this is a future battle before the Day of Judgment."[4]

On the day of my solo lunch at a French restaurant in Berkeley, I met with Hatem Bazian in his office on the Berkeley campus. When I asked him about the two quotes that have landed him on the list of dangerous academics, he rolled his eyes. "Intifada," it turns out, is nothing more than the word for "uprising" in Arabic, and he was hardly the only activist calling for an uprising against the war in Iraq.

At my mention of the second quote, a look of weary amusement crossed Hatem's face. Rumors associating him with the quote have been around for a while, and he has traced the origins of the rumor to the book *American Jihad*, by Steven Emerson. In that book, Emerson first claimed that Hatem made the statement in 1996. Later he revised the date to 1999.

In both cases he claimed that Hatem made the statement at a conference that, according to Hatem, never took place. "Even if there had been a conference, it is not a hadith I would use," Hatem told me. "It is a saying of the Prophet about the end of time. So even if I wanted to discuss that particular hadith—which I don't—I'd only talk about it as an apocalyptic vision, and not as something normative for today. I have a variety of lectures that I give around the country, and none of them have to do with the Islamic vision of the end times. But it has served the purpose of tarnishing my image."

At first glance, Hatem's image may not seem like one that anyone would want to tarnish. He's a peace activist, and his practice of Islam is strongly influenced by Sufism, a deeply mystical tradition within Islam that encourages personal piety and good works.[5] Because Sufism embraces music and poetry and other forms of artistic expression, many of Islam's more austere and militant movements—such as the Wahhabi tradition, whose followers include the Afghan Taliban and the members of *al-Qaida*—have condemned Sufism as heresy.[6]

So I asked Hatem how the gentle and kind man I knew, the Sufi with whom I had taught an interfaith dialogue class, ended up being such a threat to America. "We are living in a highly contentious period," he told me. "We have a split in our society—50 percent say it's night and 50 percent say it's day—and it's not only on the issue of Muslims, but this is true for almost any issue we have, from health care, to immigration, to the budget, to how we deal with the economy after a collapse. Within that context there is an attempt to create a foreign enemy that is in our midst. Right now, that foreign enemy is Muslim, especially a Muslim who is ready to speak out."

Hatem is that Muslim. He understands that being silent could earn him a quiet life of scholarly pursuits, but for Hatem success in academia brings with it a weight of responsibility to the broader society, an obligation to speak truth to power and to articulate peaceable and just solutions to problems that threaten the common good.

This places Hatem squarely within the tradition of academic activism that elevated the University of California, Berkeley, to a place of prominence in the geography of American academic activism. In 1964 students at Berkeley began protesting university rules prohibiting the on-campus promotion of off-campus political activity, especially civil rights activism. Students responded with a wave of protests that came to be known as the Free Speech Movement. This movement, besides being successful in efforts to secure students' rights to organize around—and to raise funds for—off-campus political activism, became a watershed moment for political activism in the United States. It attracted the attention and support of folk diva Joan Baez and served as an inspiration for later protests against the war in Vietnam. Both Edwin Meece III, as the local district attorney, and Ronald Reagan, as a candidate for governor of the State of California, successfully used their opposition to the Free Speech Movement as a stepping-stone to later success in politics.[7]

In September of 1964, as the Free Speech Movement was gathering steam, Jackie Goldberg, a Berkeley student who ended up being one of the movement's leaders, articulated an intellectual motivation for the protests: "We don't want to be armchair intellectuals. For a hundred years, people have talked and talked and done nothing. We want to help the students decide where they fit into the political spectrum and what they can do about their beliefs. We want to help build a better society."[8]

It is a statement that could have been made by Hatem, who is committed to living as a public intellectual and an activist academic, but for Hatem it is Islam more than anything else that inspires his desire to change society. "For me, religion and belief are about addressing and fixing the world I am a part of," he told me when I asked him about the role Islam plays in inspiring his activism. "For me, religion is about an ethical tapestry to operate by. The Prophetic statement 'The best of you is the best of the people' means that you have to serve and provide comfort and help for the people, and to serve people you have to serve those who are the least able in the society: the poor, the homeless, the needy, those who are oppressed, because they don't have adequate advocacy, and the Prophet says that God can be found next to those who are brokenhearted. For me, that's where I see my social justice agenda. It's part of my faith. Islam is about going out and doing the things that need to be done."

JIHAD

As Hatem was describing his work as an activist academic, it was starting to sound like jihad as the word is understood by Muslims: a personal struggle. Any book on Islam must address the concept of jihad, especially since the concept is misunderstood by most people in the non-Muslim West; but asking an American Muslim, "Are you engaged in jihad?" is not easy to do. If ever an Arabic word packed a load of politically charged emotional baggage tied down with the ropes of ignorance, it would be jihad. Stripped of its encumbrances and using a literal and secular definition, jihad just means "struggle" or "exertion," but as with many religious words, the secular and literal definitions play second fiddle to the language of faith.

Among Islam's pop-cultural detractors in the United States and in Europe, jihad, as a religious concept, is universally seen in the most negative and alarmist way possible. Daniel Pipes, for example, wrote a column for the *New York Post* in which he defined "jihad" as "holy war":

> Or, more precisely: It means the legal, compulsory, communal effort to expand the territories ruled by Muslims at the expense of territories ruled by non-Muslims.
>
> The purpose of *jihad*, in other words, is not directly to spread the Islamic faith but to extend sovereign Muslim power (faith, of course, often follows the flag). *Jihad* is thus unabashedly offensive in nature, with the eventual goal of achieving Muslim dominion over the entire globe.[9]

Pipes's idea that "jihad" refers to expanding "sovereign Muslim power" as a religious responsibility would be foreign to most modern Muslims, especially in America, where fewer than two hundred Muslims were apprehended for involvement in terrorist plots in the first decade after 9/11.[10] This number represents less than .008 percent of America's 2.6 million Muslims,[11] which is to say that a tiny minority of Muslims believe it is their religious responsibility to engage in terrorism and other forms of violence.

When Muslims do engage in terrorism, they often call it jihad, but they don't usually justify the use of the word jihad by saying that it is a religious duty to build a Muslim empire. Instead, they tend to say that they are defending the Arab homeland against Western colonialism and cultural hegemony, perhaps, or that they are fighting the injustice of autocratic secular governments (both justifications, in theory, could be grounds to engage in violent jihad). There also are Muslims who work actively to convert unbelievers to Islam, but this is not jihad: it is *da'wa*, which means "call," and refers to missionary work.[12]

This is not to say, however, that Daniel Pipes's understanding is entirely incorrect. It's not. It's just that his definition of jihad is slightly more than 1,250 years past its sell-by date. According to Zaid Shakir, whom we met in chapter 3, the idea that jihad entails a religious duty to expand the territory under Muslim control was popular in the mainstream of Islamic thought during the Umayyad caliphate, which began in 657 and lasted for 88 years. It was a time of serious and historically unprecedented territorial expansion, but it was entirely unsustainable. Shakir writes:

> The demise of the [Umayyad] "Jihad State" led to a permanent restructuring of Muslim political praxis away from a scheme of permanent warfare against non-Muslims, to one which came, over time, to include protracted truces, formal diplomatic relations, and, in the modern world, membership in the international community of nation-states. More importantly, again, in the modern world, this restructuring of Muslim political praxis has led to the implicit and explicit recognition of the institutions and regimes which collectively work to make peace, not warfare, the dominant reality governing relations between nation-states. It should be noted that this emerging praxis sometimes conflicted with the theory of "jihad as perpetual warfare," a theory that remained in many legal and exegetical writings, even though in the modern world it is a theory that does not inform the foreign policy of even the most radical Islamic state.[13]

Most modern Muslims understand jihad in personal and spiritual terms. This understanding is reflected in every book and article about Islam written by a Muslim that I have ever read. In fact, some of the most beautiful writing on Islam that I encountered while researching this book was written on the subject of jihad. An example comes from Seyyed Hussein Nasr, a professor of Islamic studies at Georgetown:

> To wake up in the morning with the Name of God on one's lips, to perform the prayers, to live righteously and justly throughout the day, to be kind and generous to people and even to animals and plants one encounters during the day, to do one's job well, to take care of one's family and of one's own health and well-being—all require *jihad*. . . . Because Islam does not distinguish between the secular and religious domains, the whole life cycle of a Muslim involves a *jihad*, so that every component and aspect of it is made to conform to divine norms.[14]

For Muslims, the idea of jihad as integral to personal piety stems, in part, from a distinction between two different kinds of jihad. This distinction dates back to the days of Muhammad: according to an oft-repeated and well-loved story, the Prophet, upon returning to his home in Medina after securing a hard-fought victory against the armies of Mecca, told his followers that, having finished the lesser jihad—meaning warfare—it was time to engage in the greater jihad, by which he meant "jihad against your passionate souls."[15]

The popular Muslim focus upon the "greater jihad" of personal piety does not mean that the "lesser jihad" doesn't exist; rather, militaristic jihad simply isn't much of a factor for the overwhelming majority of modern Muslims. Most aren't involved in armed conflict, and even for those who are, most armed conflicts don't rise to the level of jihad. According to Islamic law, in order for an armed conflict to be considered jihad, the warfare must be defensive, and the declaration of jihad must be made by appropriate and authoritative religious scholars. So jihad of the lesser sort happens, but not often, and seldom in a way that will involve the Muslim next door.

When the subject of jihad arises in conversation with the Muslims I have met, the response almost always sounds something like Hatem's answer when I asked him if his work is jihad. "Jihad is exerting maximum effort toward any intended goal," he told me, retreating to the safety of a strictly secular definition of the word. "So a person who is studying and is attempting to exert maximum effort in education is undertaking jihad. A doctor doing his best to save a sick or injured person is conducting jihad. Now, definitely, there is a jihad that involves physical combat, but that is just one part of the totality."

He still hadn't answered my original question, so once more I asked him if he was engaged in jihad. It was a hard question for him to answer. Using a strict, Islamic understanding of the concept of jihad, his work is jihad. However, most Americans don't understand what jihad means to a Muslim.

"There are problems relative to the concept of jihad," he told me. "As a Muslim I understand that there is sensitivity toward the word itself, in a similar way to how in the Muslim world, if you use the term 'crusade,' you immediately have a legitimate response in certain circumstances, but there is a valid use of the word 'crusade.' You could call persons to undertake a crusade against drugs, or hunger, or homelessness, and in the same way you can call a jihad that addresses the needs of human beings. Here we have two terms that have both a reasonable understanding and a misunderstanding when they are located purely in the political realm, and that's part of the problem—we are looking at the world purely through a political lens."

Hatem's comparison between the words "jihad" and "crusade" seems worth a moment's reflection. When Billy Graham put on massive evangelism road shows and called them "crusades," no one imagined that he intended to invade the Holy Land or attack Cathar strongholds under the banner of the cross. In the same way, when Hatem makes fighting for social justice his jihad, no one should assume he is a terrorist.

CRITICISM FROM AMERICAN SUPPORTERS OF ISRAEL

Jihad or not, Hatem's work and words have earned him a fair number of critics. It is not easy being Palestinian, Muslim, intelligent, articulate, and active in public discourse. I asked him about threats and harassment that he has received in response to his activism. "It ebbs and flows," he responded. "If I give a public lecture or speak out at a rally, I usually get threats, sometimes more, sometimes less."

Hatem has been vocal on a wide variety of issues. He has organized students around the Americans with Disabilities Act, he's worked with the sanctuary movement, he's supported immigrant rights and workers' rights, and he's been involved in efforts to address homelessness and hunger. Yet most of those who protest Hatem's work do so because they are pro-Israel and he is a Palestinian critic of Israel's policies and practices of occupation of Palestinian territories. "The pro-Israel voices are intertwined with Islamophobic voices right now," he told me. "Because of the presence of Hamas in Palestine, contesting Israel's policies, the two issues tend to collapse into one another." He then listed off his pro-Israel detractors: David Horowitz, Daniel Pipes, Robert Spencer, and Pamela Geller. "They use Islamophobia and the threat of global terror as a way to link Islam to a pro-Palestinian agenda."

Hatem's statement regarding the pro-Israel leanings of America's most prominent purveyors of Islamophobia matched my own observations while doing research for the final two chapters of this book. Although it would be grossly inaccurate to say that every American supporter of Israel is Islamophobic, the most important purveyors of popular Islamophobia in America either work directly for or receive funding from organizations and foundations—both Jewish and Christian—that advocate for Israel over and against the Holy Land's Palestinian populations.[16]

Those who write, distribute, and fund Islamophobic rhetoric do not necessarily represent the mainstream of American support for Israel. In fact, no less a mainstream pro-Israel organization than the Anti-Defamation League has spoken out against the work of Stop the Islamization of America (SIOA), an organization whose cofounders, Pamela Geller and Robert Spencer, are among the most influential leaders in America's anti-Islam movement.[17] Nonetheless, the network of individuals and institutions that promote Islamophobia, though small, is effective in its reach. Language invented and employed by such writers as Robert Spencer and Pamela Geller has been adopted by members of the media and by influential politicians in Washington.[18]

SOME FINAL THOUGHTS

As with everyone I interview, I wanted to give Hatem Bazian the opportunity to say anything that remained to be said about Islam to you, gentle reader, whom I took the liberty of describing as "most likely a Christian, and probably a Presbyterian" (please forgive my presumption if you are neither). Here's what he said: "Remember, we are the 'strangers' that you are asked to take care of, and we look at you as the strangers we need to care for. We're all traveling in this world, and we need to find ways for us to sit down and talk and know one another."

It's hard for me to imagine that either Hatem or the faith he practices can be a threat to anyone, but for those who remain unconvinced by Hatem's gracious words, I offer the city of Berkeley and its history as an inspiration of hope. In 1964, when the Free Speech Movement was gaining momentum, many people within California's establishment and across the United States were afraid that the student-led movement was part of a larger communist plot to take over America. The FBI kept files on the Free Speech Movement's leaders and placed them on a list of people to be detained without judicial warrant in the event of a national emergency.[19]

Despite the best efforts of the university's leadership, local law enforcement, the governor of California, and even the FBI, the Free Speech Movement was successful. The protestors obtained concessions on each of their demands, yet America didn't fall victim to a communist plot, and Berkeley didn't degenerate into a Stalinist dystopia. In fact, fifty years later, Berkeley is a great place to eat fine food at expensive restaurants. For all of its liberal posturing, the market economy is alive and well in Berkeley.

I suspect we have as little to fear from Islam as we had to fear from the 1960s era and the communism that activists were reported to espouse. Hatem may or may not be successful in his jihad of seeking social justice, but whether he succeeds or fails, the world in general, and Berkeley in particular, will not be worse off for his efforts.

Part 3

History

Basics: Who Was Muhammad?

According to Islamic theology, the history of the world is peopled with an unknown number of prophets, including all of the prophets named in the Jewish and Christian Scriptures. Some of those prophets, such as Moses and Jesus, also hold the elevated status of "messenger." Muslims believe that Muhammad is the last and greatest of all the prophets and messengers.

The primary reason Muhammad is held in such high esteem among Muslims is that they believe he was chosen by God to receive the Qur'an as the angel Gabriel recited it to him, and then to publish and share with others the words God revealed to him.

But the reverence in which Muhammad is held among Muslims is not limited to the role he played in bringing the Qur'an to the faithful. Muslims consider Muhammad's example to be a perfect expression of godly living; he is to be emulated by Muslims whenever possible. Muslims pray as Muhammad prayed. Men wear beards in the style of Muhammad (see my description of Imam Tahir's beard in chap. 2); domestic life is modeled after Muhammad's household; and even the Prophet's preference for cats over dogs is preserved among many Muslims to this day.[1]

Details of Muhammad's life and his non-Qur'anic teachings are preserved in collections of writings called the hadith, which means something like "report" or "tradition." There are numerous collections of hadith, and debate surrounds the authenticity of some of them. But Muslims consider the hadith—especially those hadith that are accepted universally—to be normative in matters of faith. Their honor is not equal to that of the Qur'an, but they are revered nonetheless.

A final note on the role of Muhammad in Islam: Muslims traditionally express their reverence for Muhammad by saying the words "peace be upon him" after each utterance of the Prophet's name. When writing the Prophet's name, some notation of the blessing is given (often "P.B.U.H."—as an abbreviation for "peace be upon him"—in English). The blessing of peace is afforded to all of God's prophets, including those whose stories are told in the Jewish and Christian Scriptures. At times, as a way of noting Muhammad's superior status among the prophets, Muslims will say, "God's blessing and peace be upon him." The tradition of blessing God's prophets and wishing peace upon them is a means by which Muslims remember the normative role the prophets—and especially Muhammad—must play in the life of faith, and the blessing is given in faithfulness to a directive found in the Qur'an: "God and God's angels bless the Prophet: O believers, invoke blessings upon him and greet him with a prayer of peace" (33:56).[2]

Chapter 5

FROM MUHAMMAD
OF MECCA TO RAY IN SAN JOSÉ

If you know your history
Then you would know where you're coming from.

Bob Marley[1]

TWO AND A HALF BLOCKS FROM MY HOME, AT THE CORNER
of Oakland Avenue and East San Antonio Street, on the
eastside of San José, California, there is an intersection that
offers a glimpse into what may be the future of America. The
northeast corner hosts a Vietnamese Buddhist meditation
center fashioned from what, only months before this writing,
had been a dilapidated and abandoned house. On the south-
west corner is El Pirrín, a small Mexican restaurant that, in
my opinion, serves the best *pollo en mole* north of Mexico's
Puebla state. Across from El Pirrín, on the southeast corner,

next to St. James African Methodist Episcopal Church and St. Paul's Missionary Baptist Church—two predominantly and historically black churches that have been in the neighborhood since the days when this was the only zip code in which black people could live in San José—one can find a small corner store called "Bill's Market." Despite the sound of its name, the market is run by a young Arab Muslim man named Ray.

I first met Ray in the winter of 2004, a few months after the Boston Red Sox won their first World Series since 1920. The folks at my house needed milk, and my father, who was visiting at the time, joined me as we walked down to Bill's Market. My father is, by virtue of his marriage to my stepmother, a Red Sox fan. When we brought a jug of milk to the counter, he appraised Ray's cap, which was worn urban hip-hop style, bill up and twisted 45 degrees to the left. On the cap's facade the letters N and Y, superimposed one atop the other, proclaimed an allegiance to the dreaded and despised New York Yankees.

"You guys got Damon," my father said, referring to the baffling post-World Series trade of Johnny Damon from Boston to New York.

Ray smiled. "I hate him," he said with a broad Brooklyn accent, the twinkle in his eyes betraying an unsuccessful attempt not to gloat. "I hate everything from Boston."

Since then, as the Red Sox have been replaced as World Series champs by other teams, including Ray's Yankees and the San Francisco Giants (O happy day!), I have come to a friendly acquaintance with Ray. I know, for example, that his parents emigrated from Yemen and that Ray grew up in Brooklyn, where despite the geography of baseball, he became a Yankees fan.

"What's with the Yankees?" I asked him one day as he sold beer and cigarettes and milk and cold remedies, speaking fluently in Spanish to his mostly Mexican-American customers. "Brooklyn is Dodgers country. At the very least you should be a Mets fan."

"Nah," he said, "can't root for the Mets. That's the National League."

"You believe in the designated hitter," I diagnosed, trying to hide my disdain, because I don't.

"Look, a pitcher shouldn't have to hit the ball. Some guys like to hit, and that's OK, they can be in the National League, but we treat our pitchers right."

Ray has a satellite radio on which he listens to every Yankees' game of the season. That's 162 games, plus (since this *is* the Yankees) usually the postseason as well. It turns out that Ray is more religious about baseball than he is about Islam, but still, he was glad to know that I was writing a book about the faith of his family.

"I go to the mosque sometimes," he told me. "My dad used to pray five times a day, and he tried to get me to do the same. Mostly I would go out and play basketball instead, but people need to learn about religion. It's all the same. We have different names for God and different translations of his book, but we all believe in a higher power. There's no reason we shouldn't all get along."

As a more-spiritual-than-religious man of immigrant stock who seldom attends religious services, who thinks theological thoughts but has stronger opinions about sports than he does about religion, Ray is a fairly typical American male, at least from my experience of typical American maleness. And because this chapter will be using Ray as a starting place to explore the history of

Islam, I'd also like to suggest that Ray is a typical Muslim male, which may or may not be true, but typical or not, he is part of my neighborhood's cultural ecosystem, part of the America in which I live, and he is a regular guy—as regular as any Spanish-speaking, Yankee-loving, Yemeni-American, lightly observant Muslim from Brooklyn living in San José can be. That makes him a good place to start.

FROM WHENCE CAME ISLAM?

Now, if—as I believe—the corner of East San Antonio Street and Oakland Avenue in east San José is a window into America's future, it's worth asking how Islam came into the mix, making a home in east San José across the street from a Buddhist meditation center, next door to a black church, and within earshot of drums that play for the Aztec dancers who celebrate Christian and pre-Colombian holidays on the grounds of Our Lady of Guadalupe Roman Catholic Church, where Cesar Chavez was confirmed and nurtured in the faith. California, after all, is about as far away from the place of Islam's origin as a person can get without treading water in the middle of the ocean.

The history of Islam's place in the future of America begins more than fifteen hundred years ago, on the Arabian Peninsula, not terribly far from the area where Ray's parents were born. In the sixth century, Arabia, the desert region that includes parts of the modern nations of Syria, Iraq, and Jordan as well as the Arabian Peninsula,[2] sat like a wedge between two great empires: the Sassanian Persian Empire to the east and the Byzantine, or Eastern Roman

Empire, to the west. These empires were in a state of almost constant war; although neither conquered Arabia, both vied for dominance on the peninsula because the Red Sea, which runs along Arabia's western coast, was a maritime gateway to the lucrative seafaring trade with India and Southeast Asia.[3]

Strategically, it would have made sense for an empire—either the Persians or the Byzantines or, for that matter, even the Abyssinian Empire, across the Red Sea in Africa—to conquer Arabia. But with the exception of Arabia's southern tip, which is Yemen today, Arabia was unconquerable. Its land was too arid to support an invading army, and its inhabitants too fierce and independent minded to succumb to conquest without a fight. Arabia remained independent, but not united.[4]

For the most part, the Arabian Peninsula is uninhabitable desert, but within the desert are springs—oases—which make human habitation possible. In the years before the advent of Islam, various Arabian tribes vied for control of the peninsula's oases, frequently making war upon one another. At the time of Muhammad's birth, the largest and strongest Arabian tribe, the Quraysh, held among its most important possessions the market town of Mecca. This city's water supply was meager, but it was an important trading center, and it was home to the Kaaba, one of Arabia's most important religious shrines.[5]

The religious landscape of Arabia in the sixth century was dynamic. While most Arabs practiced a form of pantheism in which the various cults focused upon the deified personifications of celestial bodies, the people of Arabia also were familiar with Christianity and Zoroastrianism through their contact with the Byzantine and Persian Empires, and with Judaism, through interaction with Jewish communities living in Arabia.[6]

MUHAMMAD

In the year 570 (or thereabouts) Muhammad ibn 'Abdullah (meaning "Muhammad, the son of Abdullah") had an inauspicious birth. Little is known about Muhammad's early life: we know he was orphaned at an early age, and we know that his marriage to Khadijah, a wealthy woman several years his senior, seems to have been happy: the couple had four daughters who survived to adulthood (at least two other children—probably boys—did not), and they were prosperous.[7]

The decisive moment in Muhammad's life, which altered the course of human history, came in 610, when he fell into a trance during prayer and began to recite words he believed to be divine in origin, delivered by the angel Gabriel:[8]

> Read, in the name of your Lord, who created:
> created man of clotted blood.
> Read, for your Lord is most generous,
> the one who taught the use of the pen,
> taught man what he did not know.[9]

It was the first bit of divine revelation that, over the course of the following twenty-two years, would become the Qur'an, the holy book of Muslims and one of humanity's greatest literary accomplishments, which is particularly amazing, since Muhammad was illiterate.[10]

Understandably, Muhammad's first response to the revelation was fear. It is, after all, not every day that a person receives celestial visitations. At the beginning, Muhammad was inclined to keep his mystical encounters to himself, but eventually he told his wife, who believed her husband to be in communication with God; Muhammad and Khadijah then approached Khadijah's cousin, a Christian monk named Waraqa. Though he never abandoned his Christianity, Waraqa agreed that Muhammad's encounters with the divine were genuine and important enough to be shared. "You are the prophet of this people," Waraqa told Muhammad. "There came to you the greatest *namus* that came to Moses. They will call you a liar and they will treat you with scorn and cast you out and fight you."[11]

It may seem odd that so eager a supporter of Muhammad never converted to Islam, but it is important to note that at first Muhammad did not intend to start a new religion. He certainly understood himself to be a prophet for the Arabs, but his mission as he understood it was to call his fellow countrymen and women to a faithfulness rooted in traditions with which they were familiar and beliefs they already understood.[12] In particular, Muhammad's faith and message were Abrahamic, meaning he clearly understood his spirituality to be rooted in the Jewish and Christian traditions. In the second chapter of the Qur'an, Muhammad recites the following words received from God:

> They say, "Become Jews or Christians,
> and you will be guided."
> Say, "But the religion of Abraham
> is rightly oriented;
> he was not an idolater."
> Say, "We believe in God
> and what was revealed to us,
> and what was revealed to Abraham, Ishmael,
> Isaac, Jacob, and the Tribes,
> and what was given to Moses and Jesus,

and what was given to the prophets
from their Lord.
We do not make a distinction
between any of them;
we acquiesce to God."[13]

Thus Muhammad embraced a strict monotheism, but he did so in a way that would be palatable to his formerly polytheistic neighbors. He called God "Allah," which is both the Arab word for "god" in a generic sense and also the title used by pre-Islamic Arabs when talking about the supreme deity in the Arabic pantheon.[14] While Muhammad's preaching clearly called his followers on to a journey of faith that traveled in closer theological proximity to Judaism and Christianity than to the polytheistic pantheism of Arabia's past, still he preserved certain practices rooted in pre-Islamic Arabian spirituality, including the practice of pilgrimage to Mecca to circumambulate the ancient Kaaba, a cube-shaped building containing a sacred rock, which may be a meteorite.[15]

The appropriation of the cult of worship at the Kaaba—and by extension the central role the city of Mecca would come to assume in Islam—worked, both for the monotheist Muslims and for polytheists hesitant to convert, because local traditions linked the Kaaba to stories found in the Bible. There were some who said the shrine was founded by Adam, restored by Abraham and Ishmael, and later corrupted by polytheists who had forgotten their religious past.[16]

As accommodating as it was, not everyone in the city of Mecca was eager to hear Muhammad's message or to convert to his new articulation of monotheism. Indeed, the new faith had many opponents, particularly among those who profited from the polytheistic cults that drew pilgrims to Mecca from all over Arabia to visit the Kaaba, which at the time was said to be surrounded by 360 idols—one for each day of the lunar calendar.[17]

This clinging to polytheism wasn't just spiritual stubbornness. In part, the reluctance to change was economic. Mecca did not have enough water to support agriculture, so it relied upon the financial benefits of trade and of religious pilgrimage, welcoming devotees of hundreds of resident deities. So there was resistance when, for example, Muhammad returned from one of his encounters with the Qur'an-giving angel with words mocking the polytheists' pantheon and proclaiming the superiority of the god of the Jews and Christians:

> You are only worshiping graven images,
> not God; and you manufacture falsehood.
> But what you worship, which is not God,
> cannot sustain you.[18]

As it turns out, Muhammad's prophetic project almost ended in disaster. During the early years of his work of proclamation, he was protected by an uncle named Abu Talib, who was one of Mecca's leading citizens and was among Muhammad's earliest followers. But in 619, in rapid succession, both Abu Talib and Khadijah, Muhammad's beloved wife, passed away.

Without the protection of his uncle and in the absence of Khadijah's support—which was both spiritual and financial—the nascent Islamic movement was in a precarious position. Many of Muhammad's followers fled to Africa, where the Christian king of Abyssinia gave them refuge. Muhammad went on the road, seeking followers from towns and villages outside of Mecca, but he had few takers.[19]

The preservation of Muhammad's following came when a delegation from a city called Yathrib invited Muhammad and his community of believers to make a home in their city. In 622, Muhammad and the believers made the roughly two-hundred-mile journey to Yathrib. That journey, later known as the *hijra*, or "emigration," would mark "year one" on the Islamic calendar. That was the year during which Islam truly came into its own as a distinct faith practiced by an organized religious community, in a city that would come to be known as Madinat al-Nabi—the "City of the Prophet," or in English, Medina.[20]

Once the Prophet and his followers became established in Medina, three important developments occurred within Islam that had a profound and lasting impact upon the new faith. First, in Medina, Islam became a community. Before, while Muhammad and his followers lived in Mecca, they were a band of believers living among nonbelievers. In Medina, the Prophet and his followers had the freedom to settle down and to organize themselves according to the dictates of faith. They established rules for themselves and built a house of prayer, a mosque in which Muhammad and his many wives made their home.

After the death of Khadijah, Muhammad became a polygamist, which was not uncommon for an Arab man of wealth and stature living in the seventh century. In fact, such arrangements were entirely normal and culturally appropriate, as was the fact that the Prophet married his favorite wife, Ayisha, when she was nine years old.

According to modern sexual mores and legal codes, the union of Muhammad and Ayisha would be a grave offense and a serious crime. Many of Islam's modern American detractors have pointed to the marriage as evidence of serious flaws in Islam's moral foundation,[21] yet those who would use Muhammad's marriage to Ayisha to criticize Islam (especially if, in the process, they are trying to make a case for Christian superiority), would do well to note that such arrangements appear in Christian history as well. Some three hundred years after Muhammad married Ayisha, Roman Catholic canon law allowed a man to marry a girl as young as seven. In 1396, joy attended the marriage of twenty-nine-year-old King Richard II of England to Princess Isabelle, daughter of France's King Charles VI, who at the time was nearly seven years old.[22] Two hundred years after the union of Richard and Isabelle, the young queen's age was considered insignificant enough to be ignored by William Shakespeare, who portrayed Queen Isabelle as an adult in *Richard II*;[23] in the Victorian era, Charles Dickens also made light of Isabelle's age, dedicating exactly 3 sentences to her in a chapter in *A Child's History of England*, which tells the story of Richard's reign.[24]

Regardless of social mores and shifting taboos, the home Muhammad shared with his wives in the Medina mosque seems to have been peaceful. Muhammad married some of his wives for love, some out of charity, and some for reasons of political expediency, and by all reports, Muhammad and his wives enjoyed each other's company. Theirs seems to have been a home of mutual respect where everyone— including the Prophet himself—participated in the domestic chores that kept the household running.[25]

THE HOUSEHOLD OF FAITH

The community of the faithful—the *ummah* in Arabic—was much bigger than Muhammad's harem, however, and the common life shared by Muhammad's followers was more than just an accident born of like-minded coreligionists living in close proximity. For Muhammad and his followers, the creation of a righteous and amicable community was mandated by God:

> Hold fast
> to the rope of God,
> everyone,
> and do not split up.
> And remember God's favor to you:
> for you were enemies,
> and God united your hearts,
> so you became brethren
> by the grace of God.[26]

In the *ummah*, members of diverse families and tribes found their unity not in ancient familial and tribal identity but in the common search for God. This was a radical shift in a culture constructed on tribal affiliation, and blasphemous among a people for whom blood ties were sacred.[27]

Yet the *ummah* survived and thrived in part by making Islam relevant to as much of life as the tribal culture it replaced. Under the new Islamic order, there was no dichotomy between the sacred and the profane. Everything was integrated into the life of faith, and everything therefore had the potential to be holy.[28] The potential of holiness extended to every person as well, including those outside the Muslim community. At first the societal boundaries of the *ummah* extended broadly enough to include Jews, Christians, and pagans. Conversion to Islam was not required, and indeed mutual acceptance was mandated;[29] theological quibbling was to be set aside in favor of pursuing a knowledge of God:

And do not contest
the people of scripture,
unless with what is better,
except those of them
who have been unjust:
say, "We believe
in what was revealed to us,
and what was revealed to you;
for our God and your God is one,
to Whom we acquiesce."[30]

This is not to say that relations between Muslims and non-Muslims were entirely smooth. In fact, in 624, in a bitter setback to what seems to have been Muhammad's vision for a transcendent religious movement that included other so-called people of the book (meaning Jews and Christians), most of the Jewish population of Medina opted out of the *ummah*, eventually taking the side of Muhammad's Meccan enemies in later conflicts.[31]

This rift seems to have caused great sadness for Muhammad. Most scholars of Islam agree that the passages in the Qur'an that seem anti-Semitic (and there are several such passages) found their inspiration not in an anti-Jewish animus on Muhammad's part, but in anger toward a particular group of people who happened to be his neighbors.[32]

Muhammad's split with the Jews of Medina seems also to have led to the second important development that occurred in Medina. In January of 624, Muhammad directed his followers to turn around and pray, not toward Jerusalem as they had during Islam's earliest years, but toward Mecca and the Kaaba, which Muhammad believed to have been established by Adam and restored by Abraham. It was, therefore, purer, for it predated the layers of religiosity that had been piled upon Jerusalem by less-than-holy Jews and Christians.[33]

THE CONQUEST OF MECCA AND BEYOND

The third significant development that occurred among Muhammad's followers in Medina was the onset of a protracted war against the city of Mecca. In 628, six years after they had been expelled from Mecca, Muhammad and his followers captured the city and dedicated its Kaaba to Islam. But as with many wars, the fighting didn't end with the achievement of the initial goal. After the conquest of Mecca, Muhammad and his followers continued their battles, and by the time Muhammad died in 632, the entire Arabian Peninsula was under Islamic rule.[34]

There is little doubt that the fighting that marked the early years of the Muslim community had a profound impact upon the development of Islam and upon Muslim spirituality. The Qur'an, for example—though it is much less violent that the Bible—contains several passages that seem clearly to be inspired by the military context of Islam's formative years, such as,

> O Prophet, rouse the believers to battle:
> If there are twenty of you
> who persevere patiently,
> they will defeat two hundred;
> and if there are a hundred of you,
> they will overcome a thousand
> of those who scoff,
> because these are people
> who do not understand.[35]

Such passages have, understandably, caused considerable concern among non-Muslims, particularly in light of the contemporary emergence of extremist Islam, which utilizes terrorism and armed conflict to further its cause.

The issue of violence in Islam is addressed elsewhere in this book (see chap. 7), but as we transition in the unfolding story of Islam to a period of prolonged warfare and conquest, it is worth noting that the Prophet Muhammad, the Qur'an, and Islam are all products of a time more violent than our own. This was an era when, as with nearly all of human history, empires rose and fell, and it was considered natural for nation-states to expand their influence and power through armed conquest. It certainly bears remembering that at the same time the Islamic Empire expanded out of Arabia, Christians were hardly living lives of pacifism. The Byzantine Empire was in a state of almost constant war as it tried to hold back the Persian Empire; in Europe the eighth century witnessed the rise of Charlemagne and the conquests that in the tenth century would be consolidated into the Holy Roman Empire. And the violence of later European Christians reached beyond Europe. The fact that I live in North America but am of European descent, speak a European language, and reside in a city founded by Spaniards and named San José in honor of Jesus' earthly father bears witness to the extent of Christian Europe's capacity for empire building and to its thirst for territorial expansion.

The followers of Muhammad were by no means unique in their desire to expand the scope of their domain. What set them apart is that when they fought (which was often), they aspired to do so under a code of ethics, a doctrine of just conduct that was unprecedented and highly evolved for its time:

> Fight for the sake of God
> those who fight you; but do not be brutal
> or commit aggression,
> for God does not love

brutal aggressors.
And kill them wherever you catch them
and drive them from where they drove you;
for civil war is more violent than execution.
But do not fight them
in the precincts of the sacred mosque,
unless they fight you there.
If they fight you, then kill them;
such is the reward of the scoffers.
But if they stop,
God is most forgiving,
most merciful.
And fight them until there is no more strife,
and there is the religion of God.
And if they stop,
then let there be no hostility,
except against wrongdoers.[36]

The pacifist in me wants to dislike a passage such as the one just quoted for its endorsement of violence; the pragmatist recognizes that if every armed conflict were conducted under such rules of proportionality, if those fighting wars attempted to avoid brutality and aggression, if warring parties honored sacred spaces and ceased bloodshed when the vanquished stopped fighting, the world would be a better place.

THE DEATH OF THE PROPHET
AND THE STRUGGLE FOR SUCCESSION

In the waning days of March 632, after making the hajj—an important observance, because on that particular pilgrimage the Prophet established the rites and customs for the hajj that Muslims have observed ever since[37]—Muhammad died peacefully at his home in Mecca. According to tradition, he breathed his last with his head cradled in the lap of

Ayisha, his favorite wife. Following local custom, his body was laid to rest beneath the floor of his house.[38] He was probably in his early- to mid-sixties.

The circumstances of the Prophet's death are deceptively tranquil. It might seem that a patriarch who established a new religion and a military leader who survived a host of battles, dying faithfully and peacefully of natural causes while being nurtured by his beloved wife, should lead to the beginning of an age of peace in which the tranquillity of a beloved man's death is resurrected as goodwill among his followers for generations to come.

But that's not what happened.

In fact, it's hard to say exactly what did happen after Muhammad died, not because the history is clouded by mystery or lost in the sands of time. In fact, everything that happened after Muhammad's death was recorded faithfully and is readily available in hundreds of sources. It's tricky to say exactly what happened after Muhammad died because the details are confusing and complex.

It seems that Muhammad died without naming a clear successor, and apparently without articulating a clear vision for what would happen after his passing.[39] For some within the believing community living on the Arabian Peninsula, Islam was identified entirely with the living prophet; others expressed a desire to continue living as a faithful community. Eventually those in the latter group chose Muhammad's lifelong friend, father-in-law, and close adviser Abu Bakr to serve as the political and spiritual leader of the Muslim faithful, but with the clear understanding that he was not a prophet.[40]

Abu Bakr's first task as the successor (or in Arabic, *caliph*) to the Prophet was to bring those Arabs who considered the Muslim experiment finished with the death of Muhammad back into the fold. This took the better part of a year, and once it was accomplished, Islam was firmly established in Arabia and has been thriving there ever since. Then in 634, with his sights set on the conquest of Syria and Mesopotamia, Abu Bakr died, and leadership of the *ummah* passed to Umar ibn al-Khattab, one of Muhammad's closest advisers.[41]

Under Umar's leadership, the Muslim armies pushed their empire north, creating a wedge between the Byzantine and Persian Empires. Within ten years of Muhammad's death, Muslim territories included most of the Fertile Crescent, Egypt, and large parts of Iran. Within twenty years the Islamic territories included everything we now call the Middle East.[42]

Umar ruled as caliph for ten years, and the rapid expansion of Islam's empire in the Middle East during his reign is an historical curiosity: despite the fact that Muslim tradition remembers the earliest armies of Islam as being composed of brave warriors with a prodigious sense of military skill and acumen (an assessment shared by a few contemporary writers who suffered under Islamic expansion), the archaeological evidence shows little in the way of destruction or bloodshed. During the early expansion of Islam, there weren't many large battles, and few villages or cities were destroyed or plundered. Rather, it seems that Arab Muslims expanded their territory at a time when the two great empires vying for control of the Middle East—the Byzantine Empire in the West and the Persian Empire in the East—were weakened and financially strained by years of warfare and were unable to resist the rising tide of Islam.[43]

Furthermore, most of the people living in what would become the Islamic heartland were used to living as subjects to foreign empires. Very little territory in the Middle East had been independent since the rise of the Roman Empire, and most areas had been subject to foreign powers since before the days of Alexander the Great. It's possible that people living in the territories conquered by the growing Islamic Empire felt little inspiration to defend their former overlords or to resist a new set of rulers.

In 644 a Persian prisoner of war attacked and killed Caliph Umar,[44] and another member of Muhammad's inner circle, Uthman ibn Affan, was elected as the third caliph.[45] For the first six years of his caliphate, the Islamic Empire continued to spread. Muslim armies conquered Cyprus and pushed the empire westward along Africa's Mediterranean coast from Egypt to Morocco, and east-ward into central Asia, including modern-day Afghani-stan and the rest of what we now call Iran.[46] However, the second six years of Uthman ibn Affan's reign were marked by growing discontent within the ranks of Islam. The rest-lessness became open rebellion, and in 656, Muslims who felt Uthman's regime was not sufficient in its adherence to Islamic doctrine assassinated the caliph, sending Muslims into a civil war. Uthman was opposed by the followers of Ali ibn Abi Talib, Muhammad's cousin and son-in-law who, as the Prophet's closest living male relative, held what many Muslims considered to be the strongest pos-sible claim to inherit the mantle of leadership within the *ummah*.[47]

But not everyone believed that prophetic succession should remain within Muhammad's family. Ayisha, the prophet's favorite wife, for example, rode into battle against the partisans of Ali, in support of Muawiyyah ibn Abi Suf-yan, a relative of Uthman.[48] Ayisha's army lost the battle but won the war. In 657 Ali submitted to Muawiyyah's rule;

shortly thereafter some of his more fanatical followers murdered Ali for going soft.[49]

The civil war, called the First Fitna in Islamic tradition (*fitna* means "causing confusion or trials and tribulations"),[50] led to two important developments in Muslim history. First, it established the Umayya family, to which both Uthman and Muawiyyah belonged, as the dynastic leaders of the Muslim world. Under the Umayyad caliphs Islamic territories expanded even further eastward into Central Asia and westward across North Africa and into Southern Spain.[51] With territory on three continents, Islam, under the house of Umayya, became a world religion, and the temporal power of the house of Islam was unrivaled anywhere on the planet.

The second result of the First Fitna is felt to this day: those whose hopes for a more faithful caliphate under the leadership of Ali did not abandon their aspirations. There was a Second Fitna in 680, in which followers of Ali (Shiah-i-Ali in Arabic) attempted an insurrection under the leadership of Ali's son Hussein. The insurrectionists were largely nonviolent. Hussein and his followers marched with their families from Medina to what now is modern-day Iraq, hoping that at the sight of the Prophet's family, the House of Islam would be inspired to reject the Umayyad dynasty in favor of a leader who was, after all, the grandson of the Prophet.

It turns out that Hussein tragically underestimated the Umayyad desire to retain power. Although Hussein's insurrectionists had not been violent, the Umayyads were, attacking and murdering Hussein's entire company on the plain of Karbala in Iraq. Hussein died not holding a weapon but cradling his infant son.[52]

Those who wanted to establish Ali and Hussein as leaders of the *ummah*—the Shiah-i-Ali—never reconciled with the Umayyad caliphs. Today we know them as the Shiite Muslims. Shiites, who make up about 15 percent of the Muslim population worldwide,[53] are found most prominently in Iran, where they constitute the majority, and Iraq, where they have experienced discrimination as a minority. Significant populations of Shiites also live as ethnic and socioeconomic minorities in other parts of the Muslim world. Ongoing tensions between Shiite and Sunni Muslims (Sunni—or "right path," meaning orthodox—is the name broadly applied to the approximately 85 percent of Muslims who are not Shiite) lie at the root of several modern conflicts, including the violence that engulfed Iraq after the United States' invasion in 2003 and the Arab Spring uprisings in Bahrain in 2011.[54]

THE RISE AND FALL OF EMPIRES

In order to understand Islam, it is necessary to understand the events of Islam's first century, at least in broad strokes. A complete reading of Islamic history wouldn't hurt either, but it is beyond the scope of this chapter and of this book. Confined, as we are, by the limits of ink, paper, and time, let us fast-forward to the twentieth century by saying only this: for 1,300 years, the history of the Islamic world was marked by the rise and fall of empires. The Umayyad dynasty fell to the Abbasid family, which expanded and strengthened the caliphate in ways that certainly must have been unimaginable to the nomadic tribesmen who first followed the Prophet from Mecca. During the tenth century the caliphate began to fall apart. The Umayyad rulers of Spain declared their independence (see chap. 6); Shiites in Persia and Sunnis in northern India also became independent. At the dawning of the second Christian millennium, Muslims from Anatolia in modern-day Turkey replaced the Abbasid dynasty, establishing what became known as the Ottoman Empire.

At this point, although the House of Islam no longer existed as a single geopolitical entity, as a spiritual community, the *ummah* stretched from the Iberian Peninsula on Europe's western edge to the Malay Peninsula in the farthest corner of Southeast Asia. As medieval European Christendom languished in what popularly is known as the Dark Ages, in the Muslim world, scholarship, arts, and sciences flourished (see chap. 6).

Over the centuries, Muslim religious, cultural, and political hegemony faced challenges in what once had been a vast empire. European Crusaders, for a time, wrested parts of the Middle East from Muslim control. In 1492, Roman Catholic forces from northern Spain conquered Muslim territories in the southern half of the Iberian Peninsula. Hindus regained control of parts of India. But for the most part, the territories that at one time made up the empire established by the followers of the Prophet remained under Muslim control until a new kind of empire emerged out of Europe and, in the middle of the eighteenth century, began to challenge Islamic dominance in lands peopled primarily by Muslims. The new empires (for indeed there were several) were made not of contiguous territories conquered by invading armies but by merchants who, with the backing of superior military technology, established colonies for the purpose of procuring raw materials to feed the industrial growth in the West and luxuries to satisfy the refined tastes of the European nouveaux riches.

The European colonies in the Muslim world were not established as a way of furthering the economic well-being of ordinary people living in places like Tripoli, Timor, or Bangladesh. European colonists arrived to exploit the natural wealth that once enriched a great empire, and when local populations objected to European mercantile exploitation, European nations dispatched armies and navies to protect European financial interests. Before long, local political control was but a fading memory that would not be refreshed, in many cases, until the latter half of the twentieth century.[55]

In this way, while the Ottoman Empire retained a remnant of the former Islamic Empire in the Middle East, France established colonial dominance of North Africa and Lebanon; Holland and Portugal set up shop in Indonesia; and England, while establishing an empire upon which the sun was said never to set, colonized Muslim lands in Egypt, parts of Mesopotamia, and all of what today is Pakistan, India, and Bangladesh. The English also colonized the port of Aden in the southern part of the country we now call Yemen. This brings us back to Ray the Yemeni American shopkeeper from Brooklyn, who loves the Yankees and chats in Spanish to his predominantly Mexican American clientele at Bill's Market, the *mercado* where he works just down the street from my house.

YEMEN

Tradition tells us that Yemen is the birthplace of the Arab people. Because Yemen, which lies on the southern tip of the Arabian Peninsula, is home to most of the arable land on the peninsula (and therefore home, historically, to its largest population), many historians make the logical assumption that as the population of Yemen grew, people moved northward into the desert areas of the peninsula. This means that many of the linguistic and cultural commonalities shared by Arabs—including many of the religious assumptions that helped to shape Islam—began in Yemen.[56] It also is safe to say that the history of Islam described in this chapter left an indelible mark on the history of Yemen.

Sitting, as it does, at the place where the Indian Ocean meets the Red Sea, Yemen is a place of strategic maritime and mercantile importance. In the centuries before the rise of Islam, the territory and its Christian and Jewish inhabitants alternated between independence and subjugation to Abyssinian and Persian imperialism. In 628 the Persian governor converted to Islam, and in 631, a year before the Prophet's death, Ali, the above-mentioned son-in-law of the Prophet, led an army of Muslims that annexed Yemen, thereby uniting the Arabian Peninsula under the banner of a new religion.[57]

Yemen's subsequent history was typical among countries in the Muslim world. It was ruled first by the Umayyad caliphs, and then by the Abbasid caliphs; by the dawn of the second Christian millennium, as the Abbasid caliphate was beginning to disintegrate, Yemen gained a certain amount of independence under the leadership of a dynasty of Shiite clerics. In 1538 the Ottoman Empire exerted its control over northern Yemen. The Ottomans stayed a hundred years and then were kicked out by local tribal militias. They returned again to northern Yemen in 1849 and retained control in the north until the end of World War I.[58] In the south of Yemen, beginning in 1618 under the auspices of the British East India Company, England established trading centers at

Mocha[59] (which became an important source of coffee for the empire upon which the sun never set) and, later, in the port city of Aden. Besides giving the Royal Navy a strategic base from which to dominate the Red Sea, the Persian Gulf, and the Indian Ocean, Aden also provided a much-needed recoaling station for ships passing through the Suez Canal in the age of steam. Eventually the British Empire appropriated the southern half of Yemen.[60]

After World War I and the fall of the Ottoman Empire, power returned to the dynasty of Shiite imams who had ruled the territory since the tenth century and whose rule had been subject to the Ottoman Empire. A military coup d'état established a secular government in 1962.[61]

Meanwhile the British Empire continued to rule the south of Yemen until communist rebels wrested control and declared independence in 1967.[62] In 1990, after a mutual recognition that the north-south division of Yemen was a foreign and colonial construct, the two countries united to form the Republic of Yemen under the leadership of Ali Abdullah Saleh, who, before the unification of Yemen, served as president of northern Yemen.[63] He ruled with increasing autocracy until the Arab Spring of 2011, when an uprising of democratic-minded Yemenis led to a negotiated end to Saleh's rule and (at least as of this writing) a decided movement toward greater freedom and democracy in Yemen.[64]

RAY

The history of Yemen is entirely intertwined with the history of Islam and the Muslim world: its imperial rise, its cultural expansion, its subjugation to European colonialism, and the emergence of independent nations throughout what once was the expansive caliphate. As is true with many postcolonial nations the world over, Yemen's wealth has tended to be concentrated in the coffers and Swiss bank accounts of a ruling elite. Ray's family—which never was part of Yemen's privileged class—began immigrating from Yemen in 1968. "It was economics," Ray told me when I asked what led his family to leave the Arabian Peninsula in favor of Silicon Valley by way of Brooklyn. "We wanted a better life, just like everyone else who comes here."

Ray's grandparents came first, followed by Ray and his parents. Over the next four decades, siblings and extended family joined the growing American branch of Ray's family. Among the more recent family members to arrive in San José are Ray's brother Sam, Sam's wife, and two children; Sam's kids go to school with my children.

Like many American-born children of immigrants, Ray has embraced American culture with something akin to a bear hug: he loves baseball, wears hip-hop clothing, speaks both English and Spanish fluently, and claims religious affiliation but attends the mosque infrequently. Yet as a child of a family of Yemeni immigrants who came to the United States to exchange poverty for economic opportunity and political stability, Ray was also formed by the history of his ancestral homeland and therefore by the history of Islam.

That Ray, as the end product of so much Islamic history, turned out to be so entirely American is a testimony to the beautiful inclusiveness of American society. It is also a reminder that, in the end, to be Muslim is not to be terribly unlike anyone else who was born in Brooklyn to immigrant parents, loves the Yankees, lives in the Silicon Valley, speaks three languages, and works at the corner market just down the street from my house.

Chapter 6

CÓRDOBA AND THE MISAPPROPRIATION OF MEMORY

Do you know, Lieutenant, in the Arab city of Córdoba there were two miles of public lighting in the streets when London was a village? . . . I long for the vanished gardens of Córdoba.

From *Lawrence of Arabia*[1]

IN THE SPRING OF 2010, CÓRDOBA BECAME AN IMPORTANT TOPIC of conversation in the United States. Córdoba is a city in Southern Spain, but in America our conversations around Córdoba had less to do with the geography of a place than with the soul of Islam, as it was made manifest in the form of Córdoba House, a large Islamic community center that a group of well-financed, moderate Muslims was planning to build at the site of a derelict Burlington Coat Factory building in Lower Manhattan, just a couple of blocks from the site of what once was the World Trade Center. According to popular opinion, in New York, and indeed in the rest of the United States, the so-called Ground Zero Mosque was an offensive idea.[2] Pundits and politicians from around the United States and across the political spectrum demanded that Córdoba House be moved or disallowed altogether.[3]

The popular resistance to Córdoba House was spearheaded by Pamela Geller, a writer that *Salon.com* has described as "a right-wing, viciously anti-Muslim, conspiracy-mongering blogger." Geller is the chief writer for *Atlas Shrugs*, which the same article on *Salon* derides as a "third-tier, right-wing blog."[4] Third-tier or not,[5] *Atlas Shrugs* has some 200,000 monthly readers, and Geller's work has had a profound effect on the way Americans think about Islam in general and Córdoba House in particular.

Geller wrote her first blog spot attacking Córdoba House on December 8, 2009, after the *New York Times* published a piece about the proposed transformation of the old Burlington Coat Factory building into the new Islamic center.[6] For six months the issue went dormant. Then, in May of 2010, after the New York City Planning Commission approved the project, Geller's attacks on the center went viral online. She appeared on mainstream media venues, and her rhetoric was emulated by right-wing pundits and politicians from Sean Hannity to Sarah Palin.[7]

So strong was the reaction to Córdoba House that even the name for the Islamic center came under suspicion. On July 21, 2010, Newt Gingrich, the former Speaker of the House of Representatives, released the following statement about the name of the proposed Islamic center:

> The proposed "Córdoba House" overlooking the World Trade Center site—where a group of jihadists killed over 3,000 Americans and destroyed one of our most famous

landmarks—is a test of the timidity, passivity, and historic ignorance of American elites. For example, most of them don't understand that "Córdoba House" is a deliberately insulting term. It refers to Córdoba, Spain—the capital of Muslim conquerors who symbolized their victory over the Christian Spaniards by transforming a church there into the world's third-largest mosque complex.

Today, some of the Mosque's backers insist this term is being used to "symbolize interfaith cooperation" when, in fact, every Islamist in the world recognizes Córdoba as a symbol of Islamic conquest. It is a sign of their contempt for Americans and their confidence in our historic ignorance that they would deliberately insult us this way.[8]

Before long, the name "Córdoba House" was changed to "Park 51," a reference, not to the former capital of Muslim Spain, but to the street address of the proposed center.

THE CÓRDOBA MOSQUE

I first read Newt Gingrich's diatribe against Córdoba a few weeks after I returned from a visit to that city. The vitriol with which he attacked the erstwhile capital of Islamic Spain came as a surprise to me, both because it seems to reflect nothing of the historical reality I encountered in Córdoba itself, and because its report of Córdoba being a code word for Islamic conquest didn't fit with anything I'd ever heard from a Muslim.

In fact, I went to Córdoba in the first place because over the years, while speaking with Muslim friends and colleagues, I have heard a refrain repeated dozens of times: "If you want an example of what it looks like when a society is built upon the precepts of Islam, don't use the Taliban in Afghanistan as your example or even the Wahhabite regime in Saudi Arabia. Instead, look to Córdoba and to the Muslim societies of Southern Spain during the Middle Ages. There you will find an example of what Islamic society is meant to look like."

And so I went to Spain.

Córdoba's old city seduced me. The buildings are well-maintained—whitewashed and trimmed with bright colors. Mostly, the architecture looks like what you'd expect in a European city close to the Mediterranean, in France or in Italy, perhaps. But ancient arabesque architectural elements are evident as well, particularly in the windows and doors of houses whose walls encircle cool patio gardens that date back to the first centuries of Islam.

Nowhere is architectural evidence of Córdoba's Muslim past more evident than in Córdoba's cathedral, and here's what's truly amazing about the Córdoba cathedral: it's also a mosque. This is not to say that Muslims are welcome to pray here in a formal way; Roman Catholicism has set down some serious roots in this place, and Catholics have claimed the sacred space with ferocity. When my friend Imam Tahir visited Córdoba with a group of Muslims a few weeks after my stay there, security guards threatened to arrest him if he tried to pray. The church is Catholic and has been for centuries, but when Catholic Spaniards expelled the local Arabic and Muslim population (the people they called the Moors) in 1236, they didn't do what the Catholic Church tended to do everywhere else when it moved in and displaced locally held religious beliefs: they didn't destroy the local religious shrine and build a cathedral on the foundations of the sacred space that had been knocked down. Instead, they built a church inside and up through the roof of the mosque, and then dedicated the entire space to Our Lady of the Assumption and made it the cathedral for the Diocese of Córdoba.

From the outside, as you view Córdoba from the Roman bridge across the Guadalquivir, it looks like the city is graced with a large Spanish Baroque cathedral. At a distance, the edifice looks like many of the churches I have seen in Latin America (a reminder that the Catholic Spaniards kicked Muslims out of Southern Spain at precisely the same time they began their conquest of territories in the New World), but upon closer inspection it becomes apparent that the cathedral rests, like a brooding dove, atop the larger, considerably shorter, flat-roofed structure that was the Córdoba mosque.

Inside the cathedral entrance, men are told to remove their hats—another reminder that this is *not* a mosque— and the visitor is greeted by hundreds of red-and-white arches that sit atop the columns supporting the mosque's relatively low ceiling. The arches are made from both brick and stone, which gives a stratified candy-cane appearance to the interior.

The repetition of the arches is like a mantra, a short, beautiful prayer repeated again and again, until it becomes bigger and more powerful than the sum of its parts. If viewed one way, the colorful arches form straight, well-ordered columns, but with a turn of the head, looking forty-five degrees to the left or to the right, they create a kaleidoscope of offset columns and curves. They dance.

I walked through this exotic—and honestly, almost erotic—space, and without warning, suddenly I was in a Spanish Baroque Roman Catholic cathedral, the cruciform ceilings soaring a hundred feet above me. The dome at the center of the transept was gilded with gold and guarded by cherubs. The high altar sparkled with all the pre-Vatican II shininess a Protestant American tourist like me hopes to see in a European Catholic church: angels and saints and candles and a choir with exquisitely carved seats facing each other across the nave. My Calvinism was silenced, and for a moment I wanted to venerate the Blessed Virgin, hear a Latin Mass, and let a communion wafer dissolve on my tongue. But I kept walking: just as quickly as the Catholicism appeared, it was gone, and I was back in the mosque. Let me try to explain this place using religious language: "There is no God but God and—AVE MARIA!—Muhammad is his prophet."

When I reached the far side of the building, I encountered what may be the most beautiful bit of sacred architecture I have ever seen, the mihrab, the point in the building that orients worshipers toward Mecca. It is an alcove behind an arched doorway. The stones inside the mihrab are light in color and trimmed with gold. Hidden skylights let in the sun, which glitters out of the doorway into the dim light of the mosque as if the mihrab is an entrance into heaven. Because construction of the mosque began in 785, which was before advances in geography enabled mosques to be built with an accurate orientation toward Mecca, this mihrab points directly south, more toward, say, Ouagadougou, Burkina Faso, than toward Mecca. But I'm glad. The mihrab's southern orientation means that sunlight illumines this celestial portal all day long; a southeastern orientation might not have the same impact.

It would be tempting to imagine that the placement of the cathedral inside the former mosque is a sign of great religious tolerance among the people of modern Córdoba—a lasting testament to the open society that for a time spread throughout Southern Spain and had as its capital and epicenter the city of Córdoba—but that would be wishful thinking. In fact, the local Catholic hierarchy seems to be doing everything it can to discourage the idea that Córdoba ever was a city of tolerance.

When I entered the cathedral grounds through a door that leads into the ancient gardens that became the cathedral cloisters, I paid my entrance fee and crossed the lovely cloisters, which boast a grove of handsome orange trees. I entered the main cathedral/mosque and picked up a tourist guide, which begins its brief history of the church with the following words: "Beneath every cathedral is always a bed of hidden cathedrals. In the case of Córdoba, tradition traces back to its Visigoth origins. . . . It is an historical fact that the basilica of San Vicente was expropriated and destroyed in order to build what would later be the mosque, a reality that questions the theme of tolerance that was supposedly cultivated in the Córdoba of the moment."[9]

Artifacts from the Visigoth church that stood on the site now occupied by the cathedral are on prominent display, and there is a hole in the floor through which a visitor can gaze down on the remains of the mosaic floor from the earliest Christian church. It is as if the local church is saying, "Don't hate us! Sure, we built a gaudy cathedral in the middle of a mosque, but they did it too. And we were here first." These protestations ring hollow because the Roman Catholic Church was not the first religious tradition to arrive in Córdoba; the city predates Christianity and Pagans worshiped on the site now occupied by the Cathedral, but never mind. History is messy, and the Roman Catholic Church is to be commended for preserving as much of the mosque as it did.

Despite the oddly superimposed cathedral, while I was in Córdoba, I saw several groups of Muslim tourists visiting what once was the spiritual heart of a remarkable Islamic kingdom. Even if, like my friend Tahir, they were threatened with arrest for praying, I doubt they went away disappointed in the architecture from Iberian Islam's golden age that is preserved in the cathedral, which used to be a mosque, which, before that was a heretical house of Christian worship, which originally was a pagan shrine.

THE MUSLIM CONQUEST OF CÓRDOBA

No one really knows how long human beings have lived in the place we now call Córdoba. According to a guidebook I picked up in one of the city's many tourist shops, by the time the Roman Empire made Córdoba the capital of its Spanish territories in 45 BCE, the city boasted a brisk economic life and twenty thousand inhabitants. For the time, that was a city of considerable size. Besides being an important regional economic and political center, Córdoba's cultural life was robust enough that one of its sons—the poet, playwright, and philosopher Seneca—earned a well-deserved reputation as one of the great Roman men of letters.[10]

In the fifth century of the Common Era, as the Roman Empire receded from the Iberian Peninsula, the Visigoths, a Germanic tribe notorious for sacking Rome in 410 CE, filled the power vacuum. The Visigoths ruled—somewhat ineffectually—over a land peopled by a diverse collection of ethnic communities—Celts, Africans, Romans, and Jews—who together created an "ethnic paella pot" in Southern Spain.[11]

The Visigoth kingdom in Spain lasted about three hundred years. The realm was as diverse religiously as it was ethnically: the ruling Visigoths practiced an Arian brand of Christianity (non-Trinitarian, believing that Christ is not coeternal but was created by the Father)[12] until the year 589, when they converted en masse to dominant Christian orthodoxy as defined by the bishop of Rome.[13] They did not, however, convince all of their subjects to share their beliefs. Alongside the alternately heretical and orthodox Christianity of the ruling class, residents of the Iberian Peninsula practiced Judaism and several varieties of paganism.[14] It was not a cohesive society.

Meanwhile, to the South and East, the Islamic Empire was on the rise. After spreading out of Arabia and conquering the Middle East and North Africa under the leadership of the Umayyad dynasty, Muslim armies looked across the Strait of Gibraltar and saw a rich and alluring land ruled by weak governors. They attacked, eventually conquering the southern half of what we now know as Spain. They named the land al-Andalus (Andalucía in modern Spanish, Andalusia in English); eventually Muslims living in al-Andalus would establish a society that was remarkable for its advances in culture and knowledge and unprecedented in its tolerance toward those who were neither ethnically Arab nor religiously Muslim.

Islamic religious tolerance was not invented in al-Andalus. The foundational teachings of Islam include a respect for the religious traditions that preceded the religion of Muhammad. In its earliest years, Islam seemed willing to embrace ideas from a wide variety of religious traditions, including various expressions of indigenous Arabian-peninsula paganism that were folded into the spiritual practice that became Islam.[15]

UMAYYAD CÓRDOBA

Insofar as intolerance marked the early years of Islam, it was the intolerance various factions within Islam had for one another. The first two hundred years of Islamic history are marked both by a dizzyingly rapid expansion of the Islamic Empire and by intrigue, assassination, and civil war. Both forces helped create Córdoba's golden era. Muslims conquered al-Andalus in 711 CE, and in the year 750 intrigue, assassination, and civil war brought an epoch of unprecedented tolerance to the southern half of the Iberian Peninsula when a young man named Abd al-Rahman arrived in Córdoba.

The Umayyad dynasty was founded in 644, just twelve years after the death of the Prophet Muhammad. In the last chapter we saw that during the dynasty's 105 years, the Umayyad rulers expanded the reach of Islam to create an empire larger than any the world had ever known. This was remarkable since the reign of the Umayyad family bore witness to almost nonstop civil war between the Umayyads and various other factions within the house of Islam.

The struggles of the Umayyad dynasty came to a close in 749 with the rise of the Abbasid family, who took control of the Muslim Empire after slaughtering the entire Umayyad family, save for a young prince named Abd al-Rahman. At the age of perhaps sixteen (no one really knows), he escaped the Muslim heartland in modern-day Syria, making his way first to Morocco, the birthplace of his Berber mother, and then across the Strait of Gibraltar and into the farthest limits of the Muslim Empire.

When the young prince reached al-Andalus in the year 755, the territory was in disarray resulting from infighting among inept and corrupt officials. Within a year Abd al-Rahman mustered an army of supporters, overthrew the local emir, or governor, and established himself as emir of Córdoba and all of al-Andalus. It is remarkable that so young and inexperienced a prince—the only surviving member of his family, arriving alone and unannounced in an unfamiliar land—could accomplish so swift a coup, but the secret to his success may have been the very mystique generated by his survival. That the government in al-Andalus was a mess didn't hurt his chances either.

In short order Abd al-Rahman established himself as a force with which to be reckoned. The emir tried to buy time by offering the young prince his daughter's hand in marriage. It didn't work. In May of 756 Abd al-Rahman led an army to victory in a battle outside Córdoba. The conquering prince took control of al-Andalus, thereby altering the course of Western history.[16]

Technically, Abd al-Rahman and his descendants were subject to the Abbasid regime, which had moved the capital of the empire to Baghdad (it would be 200 years before a descendant of Abd al-Rahman would declare al-Andalus an independent caliphate). But for the most part, the Umayyads living in Córdoba ruled over an autonomous state in what is today Southern Spain. Their reign there lasted more than three hundred years, during which time a remarkable society took shape, thanks to the political stability provided by the dynasty.[17] During the three centuries of Umayyad domination in Southern

Spain, hydrological engineers developed the most technologically advanced irrigation systems in Europe, allowing the semiarid landscape to produce an abundance of crops. Many of these foods were unfamiliar to Northern Europeans—citrus and watermelon, spinach and asparagus. Hydrological advances and the economic prosperity that flowed from them allowed Córdoba's population to indulge in the luxuries of deodorant and bleach at a time when Northern Europeans seldom bathed or did their laundry.[18]

The political stability and economic prosperity of Southern Spain under the leadership of the Umayyad dynasty enabled Córdoba to become the most important center of learning in its day. At the turn of the second millennium, for example, Pope Sylvester II was occasionally suspected of being a practitioner of black magic due to the speed with which he could calculate complicated mathematical problems without using pen or paper. But the pope was not a wizard. As a young man he had visited Córdoba, where he learned to use Arabic numerals instead of Roman ones; while every other European wanting to calculate the number of seconds in a year, for example, would have to do so by multiplying LX by LX by XXIV by CCCLXV, Pope Sylvester could multiply $60 \times 60 \times 24 \times 365$, which is far easier.[19]

Advances in hygiene, agriculture, and mathematics notwithstanding, the crowning cultural achievement of Córdoba (and indeed of Muslim Spain) may have been the gathering unto Córdoba of a remarkable collection of books. Although a well-stocked library in Northern Europe around 1000 CE may at best have had four hundred books, the libraries in Córdoba had hundreds of thousands of volumes, including vast numbers of Greek philosophical works that were translated into Arabic.[20]

JEWISH CÓRDOBA

When I was in Córdoba, I looked for, but couldn't find, the buildings that once housed the city's collection of books. A thousand years later, the buildings may or may not have survived, but they were not mentioned in the guide to the city I purchased, and no one I asked seem to know where they were. What I did find, however, was Córdoba's venerable synagogue, which dates back to the opening decades of the thirteenth century. It is one of three surviving synagogue buildings that predate the so-called *reconquista* or "reconquest,"[21] when in 1492 the armies of King Ferdinand of Aragon and Queen Isabella of Castile united the nation we now call Spain.[22]

It's not entirely accurate to say that Jews living in Southern Spain under Umayyad rule had no problems, or that their Muslim overlords always minded their own business, allowing the Jewish community to thrive economically, practice the Jewish religion, or express Jewish culture on Jewish terms.[23] Like their Christian counterparts, Jews as "People of the Book" living under Muslim rule, were *"dhimmi,"* a protected class of people, but the protection came at a cost. Jews and Christians were required to pay an extra tax[24] for the privilege of living as second-class (in the case of Jews) and third-class (in the case of Christians) citizens;[25] no doubt this protection at times felt like extortion. It is safe to say, however, that Muslims in Córdoba and elsewhere in Southern Spain were more tolerant and accommodating of religious diversity than were Christians elsewhere in medieval Europe. While the Jewish population in al-Andalus enjoyed relative prosperity and privilege, Christian kings and magistrates in Europe passed laws restricting the kinds of employment available to Jews, forced Jews to live in ghettos, outlawed conjugal relations between Christians and Jews, forbade Jewish women from serving as wet nurses for Christian children, and blamed Jews for everything from the death of Christ to the plague.[26]

In creating a society that afforded Jews with relative freedom, Córdoba was not unique in the Muslim world, nor were the medieval years the only era of Jewish well-being under Islamic law. In fact, Jews tended to fare better in the Islamic world than in Christian societies up until the twentieth century. Although anti-Semitism certainly is present in modern Muslim societies—much of it expressed in response to the creation of Israel and to Israel's subsequent occupation and settlement of Palestinian lands—it's interesting to note, as has the British scholar Karen Armstrong, that most of the anti-Semitic images and tropes currently in use in the Muslim world have been imported from Christian Europe.[27]

What is remarkable about the acceptance shown to the Jewish communities in al-Andalus is that it outlasted the Umayyad dynasty in Córdoba. No one knows for sure when the first Jews arrived in Southern Spain, but their presence on the Iberian Peninsula dates back at least to the early years of the Common Era.[28] Under the laws of the Roman Empire (which lasted in Southern Spain until the fourth century, when the Visigoths displaced the Romans), Jewish communities never were free from persecution; after the Visigoths conquered the Roman territories in Spain, things only got worse. Among other repressive measures, Visigothic kings outlawed circumcision, the keeping of the Jewish Sabbath, and the observation of Jewish holy days. Jews were subject to forced conversion and were kept from full participation in the economic life of what would become Spain.[29] Following the Arab conquest of al-Andalus, life for the Iberian Jewish community started looking up.

Jews in Muslim Spain could also hold positions of prominence. As a numeric minority, Arabs were unable to staff all of the government offices with Muslims. Because they feared that Christians placed in positions of authority might usurp power from their foreign conquerors, Muslims tended to appoint Jews to jobs in civil government throughout their territories in Southern Spain. As a result, Jews were to be found not just among the ranks of civil servants, but also among Islamic Spain's most important scholars, merchants, and artisans.

THE FALL OF MUSLIM SPAIN

In 1013 the unity of Islamic control over Southern Spain was broken when Córdoba fell to an army of Moroccan Berbers whose take on Islam was several degrees less tolerant than that practiced by their Umayyad predecessors.[30] The unity of Muslim al-Andalus would never be restored, and the former caliphate broke up into smaller kingdoms.[31] In 1236 Ferdinand III of Castile wrested control of Córdoba from its last Muslim rulers.[32] He was the first Spaniard to control territory in Southern Spain since before the Roman Empire, and the first Christian since the waning years of the Visigothic Empire.[33]

The fall of Muslim Córdoba—first to the Berbers and two centuries later to Christians from the north of Spain—signaled the beginning of the end of Islam's dominance in al-Andalus. Over the course of two hundred years, Spanish Christendom chipped away at what once was a great caliphate. The waning years of Muslim Spain still saw great moments of enlightenment and cultural progress: this was the era when Jews living in Spain added to and developed the Kabbalah, for example.[34] But as all nations and empires must one day come to an end, so too, beginning with Córdoba's demise, the flame that was the Muslim Empire on the Iberian Peninsula first flickered, then sputtered, and then went out altogether.

THE RISE AND FALL OF EMPIRES

All the best evidence notwithstanding, a significant portion of Americans have adopted an understanding of Córdoba's place in history that is influenced more by the Pamela Gellers and Newt Gingriches of the world than by reflective scholarship. This can be frustrating for those of us who wish to engage in informed conversation set free from the constraints of fearful rhetoric. Yet on one point, those who interpret the legacy of Córdoba in a negative light are correct: Córdoba was, for hundreds of years, the regional capital of a foreign, conquering empire, which brought a new religion, an alien language, and strange cultural norms to Southern Spain. This is a fact that bears some consideration. After all, even if the Muslims brought a heretofore-unknown level of religious tolerance, and even if the learning associated with medieval Córdoba surpassed anything the world had ever seen, still the Muslim rulers of Southern Spain were a foreign, conquering power. Should that not make a difference in how we understand them today?

In the modern era, when empires tend to be seen in a negative light, the Muslim rulers of al-Andalus do seem guilty of the wholesale plunder of other people's property and of the occupation of territory they had no right to visit, let alone appropriate into a caliphate whose growth seemed unstoppable. But it's probably worth noting that the Muslims who built the empire that grew to include al-Andalus did not invent the idea of empire. In fact, the Islamic Empire that stretched from Spain to India—though it was the largest empire the world had ever seen—was only one in a long succession of empires that rose and fell over that part of the world beginning with the Mesopotamian territorial expansions of the Sumerians thousands of years before followers of the Prophet ever set their eyes upon the city by the banks of the Guadalquivir. The fact that I wrote these words in San José, California, at a café near the corner of San Carlos Street and the Alameda, a stretch of road that is part of El Camino Real—the royal highway that once connected the Spanish missions and military outposts between Mission San Bruno in Baja California, Mexico, to Mission San Francisco Solano in Sonoma, in the heart of California's wine country—is evidence that Muslims were not the last empire builders the world has ever seen. Theirs would not be the largest empire in human history, and they weren't even the last great empire associated with Spain.

All empires control their client states and conquered people using power and violence. That the Islamic Empire to which Córdoba was connected also asserted itself using power and violence does not make that empire unique. What seems to be distinct about Córdoba and the empire it represents in the American psyche is its ability to conjure up fear among contemporary Americans. Few Americans worry about Greeks rebuilding their empire; nor do we concern ourselves with the possibility of Rome stretching its imperial talons once more; if we fear the Persians, it is because we suppose Iran might be building a nuclear bomb and pointing it in the general direction of Tel Aviv. We don't lose sleep over the possibility that anyone might try to reestablish the realm of Xerxes.

Nor does the possibility of a resurgent Spanish Christian empire cause fear, but maybe it should. On my last day in Córdoba, I visited La Galeria de la Tortura, the Torture Gallery, near the old city's Jewish Quarter. It is a museum that boasts Europe's largest collection of instruments of torture. Most of the museum's pieces were invented by Spanish Catholics for use in the inquisition against Jews, Muslims, heretics, and women suspected of practicing witchcraft; nothing in the dim and horrific displays came from Spain's Muslim overlords. One must be careful not to draw too many conclusions from a casual, accidental visit to a museum, but still, it feels safe to observe that the years of Islamic dominance in the Iberian Peninsula predated the darkest, most violent era of European history.

Part 4

Misconceptions

Basics: What Is the Qur'an?

Here is a conversation I've had with Muslim friends on a couple of occasions:

<blockquote>

BEN: So I read the Qur'an.

MUSLIM FRIEND: (*smiling enthusiastically*) Ben, that's fantastic. Tell me: what did you think about it?

BEN: Beautiful. I liked the Qur'an. It's a lot like the Bible.

MUSLIM FRIEND: (*after a brief period of pained silence in which disappointment is palpable*) Well, you didn't read it in Arabic. If you read it in Arabic, you would discover that there is a difference between the Bible and the Qur'an.

</blockquote>

In the course of my various associations with Muslims, this conversation has confused me more than any other.

In comparing the Bible to the Qur'an (also spelled Koran and Quran in English) I was committing a faux pas, but it didn't make any sense to me. By saying the Qur'an is like the Bible, I was bestowing upon the Qur'an the highest possible compliment a Christian can give to a book. It was an honest compliment and, from my perspective, an appropriate comparison. The Qur'an is a beautifully written book. It is elegant in the English versions I have read, and it sounds haunting in Arabic, even to someone like me who doesn't understand the original language. When recited aloud, the Arabic of the Qur'an—and for Muslims the Qur'an really only can be read in Arabic—has a rhythm and cadence that are mesmerizing. The appeal of the Qur'an is apparent.

In English the Qur'an reads like the book of Psalms. It is written in verse and divided, like the Bible, into chapters (or suras) and verses (or ayas). Much of the Qur'an's 114 suras and more than 6,000 ayas are dedicated to praising God using phrases and words that are entirely comfortable to a Christian. In fact, on a couple of occasions, I have used passages from the Qur'an liturgically in worship services at my church; no one in my congregation noticed.

Significant portions of the Qur'an tell stories that are found in Jewish and Christian Scriptures. Often the details of the stories are different, and sometimes the Qur'an tells stories not found in the Bible about biblical characters such as Abraham and Ishmael. It gives the Qur'an a familiar feeling for a Christian who reads the book with an open mind.

From a Muslim perspective, however, the Qur'an cannot be compared to another book, even if that book, like the Bible, is considered divine revelation. For the Muslim, the Qur'an is absolutely singular. According to tradition, Muhammad—then an illiterate businessman living in the city of Mecca—started receiving the words of the Qur'an from the lips of the angel Gabriel in the year 609. He continued periodically to receive angelic revelations until his death in 632. He recited the revealed words to his friends, who wrote them down; within twenty years of the Prophet's death the entire Qur'an was standardized and has remained unchanged ever since.[1]

Muslims believe the Qur'an is God's word not so much in the way that Christians believe the Bible is God's word, but more like the Christians believe Jesus is the Word, the *logos*, the fullest expression of the mind of God. The revelation of the Qur'an isn't just a matter of printed words. The Qur'an reveals something of God's presence. This isn't to say the Qur'an is an incarnation of God—Muslims don't worship the Qur'an itself—rather, God's presence in the Qur'an is profoundly sacramental. It is a miraculous communication of God's self.[2]

This is why it's such a problem for Muslims when fanatical American preachers decide publicly to burn the Qur'an. If someone were to burn a Christian Bible, many Christians wouldn't worry too much about it. It's not a nice thing to do, but the Gideons will bring another one. For Muslims, to desecrate the Qur'an is to disrespect the very presence of God.

Chapter 7

ISLAM AND VIOLENCE

Why do you see the speck in your neighbor's eye, but do not notice the log in your own eye? Or how can you say to your neighbor, "Let me take the speck out of your eye," while the log is in your own eye? You hypocrite, first take the log out of your own eye, and then you will see clearly to take the speck out of your neighbor's eye.

Jesus, in Matthew 7:3–5

I SUSPECT THAT EVERY AMERICAN OLD ENOUGH TO BE AWARE of what was happening remembers the morning of September 11, 2001, and the moment he or she first heard that a small band of well-organized Muslim terrorists wielding box cutters had commandeered four airplanes—two of which crashed into the twin towers of the World Trade Center in New York, one of which slammed into the Pentagon, and one of which fell out of the sky and into a field in rural Pennsylvania.

I was in bed when the voice of Bob Edwards, erstwhile host of National Public Radio's *Morning Edition*, woke me up through the speaker on my clock radio about twenty minutes after the first plane hit the World Trade Center. My wife had already left for work, so I stayed in bed alone, listening to the story unfold. More planes crashed; buildings fell. Rumors were everywhere.

Within weeks our nation was at war. American armed forces attacked Afghanistan and embarked on a "War on Terror" that has yet to abate more than a decade hence. In the wake of that September morning, besides going to war in Afghanistan, the United States invaded and occupied Iraq, a nation that had not been at all involved with an attack of any kind against the United States. Covert American operatives established a network of secret prisons—so-called black sites—to house and interrogate suspected terrorists, sometimes resorting to "enhanced interrogation techniques" such as waterboarding, despite the fact that such tactics are considered to be torture under the Geneva Conventions.[1] When the CIA desired unambiguous torture, it chartered airplanes to fly suspects to friendly countries unconcerned by the restrictions of international law, thereby outsourcing torture.[2] At a prison located within Guantanamo Naval Base in Cuba, terror suspects were incarcerated for years without trial. Some of the prisoners were under the age of eighteen,[3] and many were imprisoned on the flimsiest of evidence.

According to a report in *The Independent*, as of September 2006, "the war on terror—and by terrorists—[had] directly killed a minimum of 62,006 people, created 4.5 million refugees and cost the US more than the sum needed to pay off the debts of every poor nation on earth."[4] These are conservative estimates. The British medical journal *The Lancet* studied mortality in postinvasion Iraq and found that as of July 2006, there had been an estimated "654,965 . . . excess Iraqi deaths as a consequence of the war. Of postinvasion deaths, 601,027 . . . were due to violence, the most common cause being gunfire."[5]

That *The Lancet* could arrive at a number of casualties more than ten times that of *The Independent* speaks to the difficulty of knowing with certainty how many people have perished over the course of the War on Terror. We may never know for sure, but it is safe to say that the loss of human life has been immense.

During the decade-long War on Terror, there has arisen in the United States a mythic[6] narrative that equates Islam with all that is violent, oppressive, repressive, and vile. The myth is supported by videos like *Obsession* (see chap. 9), which has gained popularity outside mainstream distribution. However, an "Islam is evil" motif makes regular appearances in a wide range of mainstream media as well,[7] in popular entertainment, such as the Fox television show *24*, and in a host of violent video games.[8]

THE SHORES OF TRIPOLI: A HISTORY OF AMERICAN ISLAMOPHOBIA

Though it experienced a renaissance in 2001, American anti-Muslim animus was not invented in the wake of the terrorist attacks of September 11. In fact, the myth of Muslim violence is one of America's oldest popular stereotypes. In the seventeenth century in New England, prominent preachers such as Cotton Mather and his father, Increase Mather, peppered their sermons with anti-Muslim invective.[9] They were perhaps inspired by the anti-Islamic references in John Calvin's *Institutes of the Christian Religion*, and their sermonizing came at a time when Muslim pirates sailing out of North Africa's Barbary coast were attacking British shipping interests, taking British and North American prisoners, and holding them as hostages and as slaves.[10]

In the eighteenth century, after the British Navy had made peace with the Barbary pirates, some leaders of the Great Awakening, including George Whitefield and Jonathan Edwards, continued the tradition of preaching against what they considered to be the sinful deceptions of Islam. During this time, publishers in England and in the United States released dozens of books and tracts that condemned Islam, usually resorting to the same kinds of stereotypes that remain in use today—particularly those that exaggerate Muslim tendencies to engage in violence to subjugate women.[11]

In 1784—a year after the United States won independence from England, and after North American ships no longer had the protection of peace agreements between Britain and the Barbary States—North African piracy against American shipping resumed. A group of Barbary pirates captured an American-flagged merchant ship, the *Betsy*, sailing out of Philadelphia under the command of James Erwin and en route from Cádiz to Tenerife.[12] *Betsy* was the first of dozens of ships to be captured by Barbary pirates over the course of more than twenty years, but the corsairs who seized the *Betsy* and other American merchant vessels were not pirates in the popular imagination of the word. They were not mere criminals, operating independently as they pillaged ships on the high seas. Rather, the Barbary pirates engaged in what today we might call "statesponsored terrorism." They sailed under the authority of letters of marque—official, state-issued licenses to engage in piracy against American vessels—from the Barbary States, and with the tacit approval of England, whose navy controlled the waters off North Africa.[13]

By taking American merchant ships, the Barbary States were interested in more than mere booty. They hoped to receive ransom and ongoing payments of tribute before granting the safe passage of American shipping. It was extortion on the high seas. England, by countenancing the capture of American ships, hoped to thwart American designs on a place of prominence in a world economy operating under heretofore-unknown principles of free trade.[14]

Piracy off the shores of North Africa led to the United States' first international military engagement,[15] helped to establish the United States as a world power, and had a profound impact upon the way Americans view Islam. In the days when Barbary pirates terrorized the United States' nascent shipping industry, Islam was nearly nonexistent in North America among free persons. As a result, popular tales of Americans suffering at the hands of cruel buccaneers became, for many Americans, their only source of knowledge about Islam. Islam increasingly was viewed not just as an international rival for power or a false religion, but also as an evil force whose destruction would correspond with Jesus' second coming.[16] Some of these perceptions of Islam continue in America today.[17]

THE CATHAR WARS

To be fair, the myth of Muslim violence is not entirely disconnected from historical reality. For centuries, Muslims built and maintained vast empires by using the violence of military force. That violence was particularly intense along the borders, where Muslim territories abutted Christian lands in Europe. Over the centuries Muslim empires have had every kind of ruler imaginable; some of those potentates were violent. Later the Barbary pirates—like all pirates—were brutal; in their quest for power and money, they made life hell for seafarers in the Mediterranean and beyond.

This legacy of violence continues into the twenty-first century. The Muslim men who attacked the United States on September 11, 2001, were terrorists, as are the Muslim members of dozens of terrorist organizations spread throughout the world. It may seem reasonable, then, to ask why Islam fosters violence. But as a Christian well aware of Jesus' warning against seeing the speck in my brother's eye without noticing the log in my own eye (Matthew 7:3), a prior question first must be addressed: Why does *Christianity* foster violence?

Why indeed? To ponder that question, I did what everyone should do, if able, while thinking on life's more complicated conundrums. I went to the south of France.

Béziers, in the Languedoc region of France, is everything that I, a tourist from northern California, want France to be. I arrived by train from Toulouse, through wheat fields and acres of blooming sunflowers. As the wheat and sunflowers gave way to the vineyards, whose yield would end up in millions of bottles of Vin de Pays d'Oc, I saw the impressive castle at Narbonne. Ah, Europe!

At night, in Béziers, I saw beautiful French people at tables on the sidewalks, eating wonderful food in the languid night. They were engaged in conversations that seemed fraught with meaning and infused with substance. People were smoking. Their dogs were well behaved. Men weren't afraid to wear capri-length linen slacks.

It's easy to get disoriented in Béziers' old city. Like the old city in Jerusalem, Béziers' old city is a neighborhood built by Crusaders after they had sacked and destroyed the city that existed before they arrived. The result of the rebuilding is a warren of narrow streets that don't seem to go anywhere in particular. The Crusaders, it appears, were better at waging war than they were at city planning—not that I would want either city to be laid out in a way that makes more sense to me. In fact, I'm a sucker for places like Béziers, with its cobblestone streets and buildings that, on the ground floor, are home to chic boutiques and galleries, above which are apartments for those lucky enough to call this city their home.

As I explored Béziers, peeking sideways into the lives of its residents, I found myself fantasizing about living in France. I imagined my children speaking French. I longed to eat croissants for breakfast and baguettes *au fromage* for lunch. I wanted to drive an old Citroën. With my thoughts occupied by Francophile fantasies, I got lost. Naturally.

I came to Béziers to visit Cathédrale Saint-Nazaire-et-Saint-Celse, which is situated at the highest point in the hilltop city. It has a commanding view of the Orb River as it wends its way through the fields of the Languedoc, and of the Canal du Midi as it meanders northwest through fields and vineyards to Toulouse, and eventually to the Atlantic Ocean. The current cathedral in Béziers dates back to the thirteenth century. It was built atop the ruins of an earlier cathedral, which bore witness to an extraordinary act of religious violence: in a single day (July 22, 1209) an army of Crusaders slaughtered nearly twenty thousand civilians. The massacre was part of the Albigensian Crusades,[18] a twenty-year effort to destroy the Cathar heresy. This movement had taken hold in Occitania, a region that encompassed what we now know as the south of France as well as adjoining parts of Spain and Italy.

So successful was the crusade against the Cathars that almost no record of Catharism remains. The only clues to the beliefs—deemed so offensive to the Roman Catholic Church that they inspired a crusade—are those written down by opponents who were determined to stamp out any memory of the heresy. From these writings we can surmise that the Cathars adhered to a dualistic Gnosticism, believing creation to be governed by two equally powerful gods, one good and one evil. According to Cathar theology, the physical realm was the domain of the god of evil and darkness, and therefore all the pleasures of the flesh were to be avoided. So strict, it seems, was the Cathar rejection of carnal enjoyment that the most devout among them were vegetarians—not so much to shun the pleasures of eating meat but to avoid contamination from any food conceived in sexual congress.[19]

The Cathar rejection of what had become accepted as Christian orthodoxy seems to have rested on the idea that the Roman Church was established by the god of all evil in an attempt to frustrate the work of Christ, who—incidentally—neither died nor rose from the grave. In Cathar theology, both death and resurrection are only possible for those who are alive in a corporeal—and therefore evil—way.[20]

This is not to say that the population of the south of France, under Cathar influence, renounced fleshly pleasures universally. Roman Catholicism remained strong in Occitania in the years leading up to the Albigensian Crusades, and even among the Cathars strict asceticism was practiced only by the so-called perfecti, or "perfect ones" (also called bonnes hommes, "good people"). These men and women, after entering the ranks of Cathar clergy, chose to renounce the pleasures of the flesh and pursue lives dedicated to religious devotion. The Cathars who were not among the perfecti, meanwhile, lived lives that were socially and culturally indistinct from their Roman Catholic neighbors.

As Catharism flourished, the growth of Cathar adherents, especially among the wealthy and landed class in Occitania, became a source of growing alarm within the Catholic hierarchy. Starting in the twelfth century, a succession of popes started sending missionaries to the south of France in the hope that the Cathars might be won back to Catholicism through persuasion. Notable among the missionaries were Bernard of Clairvaux (later Saint Bernard), who began his work among the Cathars in 1145; and Domingo Guzmán (later Saint Dominic), whose monastic order (later called the Dominicans) arrived in France with members of the Franciscan order in 1206, under direction from Pope Innocent III (pope from 1198 to 1216), to bring errant Cathars back into the Catholic fold.[21] When it became clear that missionary efforts would be unsuccessful, the pope declared a crusade and offered complete indulgence to anyone willing to shed Cathar blood under the sign of the cross.[22]

The sacking of Béziers was the first serious military engagement in Pope Innocent III's crusade against heresy, yet many—if not most—of the people killed on July 22, 1209, were Catholics. While it was possible to identify the men and women who had entered into the ranks of the perfecti (they wore distinctive robes), rank-and-file Cathars looked exactly like their Catholic neighbors, so the Crusaders simply killed everyone in Béziers. "Kill them all," instructed Arnaud Amaury, the Cistercian abbot who led the attack on Béziers. "God will recognize his own."[23]

According to one eyewitness, a participant in the slaughter,

> The lords from France and Paris, laymen and clergy, princes and marquises, all agreed that at every castle the army approached, a garrison that refused to surrender should be slaughtered wholesale, once the castle had been taken by storm. They would then meet with no resistance anywhere, as men would be so terrified at what had already happened. . . . That is why they massacred them at Béziers, killing them all. It was the worst they could do to them. And they killed everyone who fled into the church; no cross or altar or crucifix could save them. . . . They killed the clergy too, and the women and the children. I doubt if one person came out alive. God, if it be his will, receive their souls in Paradise![24]

As the crusader army approached, the citizens of Béziers offered only token resistance, and the invaders went on a rampage. The city's entire population was slaughtered, many of them in churches, including hundreds who perished in the cathedral. "Surely," they must have thought, "no Catholic army will kill faithful Christians who are attending mass in a duly consecrated sanctuary." After all, since the turn of the fifth century, the Roman Catholic Church had considered its worship spaces to be places of sanctuary, safe from persecution and violence.[25] However, the citizens of Béziers who thought they could find sanctuary in the city's churches were wrong.

On a hot Sunday morning in July—a day probably not unlike the day when Béziers was sacked 801 years before my arrival—I climbed the hill leading to Béziers' old city to worship at the rebuilt cathedral. As I walked through the city's awakening narrow streets, swallows darted in and out of the spaces between the buildings above my head as café owners set out tables and chairs for the day. On so tranquil a day, it was hard to imagine what must have unfolded on those same streets, the cobblestones awash with the blood of innocents as a marauding army of northerners conducted an indiscriminate slaughter in the name of God and his church. Yet that is part of the terror of war: in only a moment, a peaceful town like Béziers can bear witness to unimaginable horror.

But there was no evidence of a crusade on the morning I got lost walking to Béziers' cathedral, and it's not just that the air was sweet and the sun was warm. I saw almost nothing that called to mind the carnage inflicted on the town during the Cathar wars. At least, that is how it seemed until I got to the cathedral itself. There I saw that the plaza in front of the church was named—without any interpretation—Plan des Albigenses (Cathar field) but more tellingly, the church built to replace the one destroyed by the Crusaders was made to look like a fortress. The cathedral in Béziers has no spires, only bell towers that look like battlements, and the massive front doors are guarded by balistrarias, or arrow slits. The whole building was designed as if to assure worshipers that the church never again would allow an invading army to kill the faithful, but I'm not sure the promise was directed at the descendants of the victims of the crusaders' attack on Béziers. I'm not sure there *are* any direct descendants of that massacre. Besides, when I arrived at the cathedral, it was early, so I took a walk through the cloisters and the cathedral garden, where for the first time I noticed the emblem for the city of Béziers, printed on a tourist information poster. It depicts a knight on horseback over the words *Béziers: L'Esprit de Conquête,* or "Béziers: The Spirit of Conquest." Béziers, it turns out, is not a city that dwells on past injustice. Nor does it hold the crusader forebearers of the current citizens in low esteem.

The cathedral bells, hidden somewhere up among the battlements, called the faithful to mass. We entered through a side door, under a bas-relief depicting the martyrdom of the church's patron saints, Nazarius and Celsus, two first-century evangelists who lost their heads after refusing to offer sacrifices to the Roman gods. The bas-relief is so graphic in its depiction of the saints' decapitation that it would surely be given an R rating if it were a movie.

Although the exterior of the cathedral is somewhat dilapidated—with plants growing between the bricks and most of the gargoyles worn to nubs by the erosion of wind and rain, frost and time—the inside is beautiful, with soaring vaulted ceilings and sparkling stained glass. As I entered the nave, a hidden organist was playing a prelude on a massive organ. The acoustics were so vibrant that I felt as if I were in the sound box of a Stradivarius; in the Béziers cathedral, the rocks sing, though not necessarily in remembrance of the victims of the Cathar wars.

WELCOME TO THE INQUISITION

The sacking of Béziers was not the first or the worst example of Christian Crusader brutality. Already 110 years before the Catholic army assaulted Béziers, soldiers of Christ under the leadership of Godfrey of Bouillon, and at the behest of Pope Urban II, destroyed Jerusalem in a gruesome bloodletting. At least twice as many people as were slaughtered in Béziers perished at the hands of Pope Urban's Christian holy warriors in 1099.[26] A similar massacre took place in 1204, when a crusading army, unable to retake Jerusalem from Muslim forces that had repossessed the city, turned their fury upon the city of Constantinople. It was, according to English religious historian Karen Armstrong, "one of the great crimes of history." Over the course of three days, Crusaders raped and murdered the citizens of the Byzantine capital while plundering the city's considerable wealth and desecrating its churches.[27]

If the annihilation of Béziers was neither unprecedented in its destruction nor unparalleled in its devastation, it was the first major battle in the Albigensian Crusades, a war whose legacy would last through centuries of Europe's religious landscape. Alongside the military campaigns of the Albigensian Crusades, which ended in a massacre of Cathars holed up in the mountain stronghold of Montségur in 1244, there arose a nonmilitary campaign of religious persecution that left an indelible mark on the European soul. That campaign was the Inquisition.

Christian intolerance of dissident theology and spirituality was not invented as a response to the Cathar heresy; for hundreds of years, dissenting and competing beliefs had been suppressed by local bishops. But when the local enforcement of orthodoxy failed to check the growth of Catharism in Europe, the Vatican decided to engage in a more top-down approach, beginning—but not ending—with two decades of bloody holy war. In 1233, four years after the conclusion of the crusades, the temporal power of Catharism had been broken, but pockets of Cathars continued to practice their faith in secret communities scattered throughout Europe. In response to this, Pope Gregory IX (pope from 1227 to 1241) established the *Inquisitio haereticae Pravitatis Sanctum Officium*, or "Holy Office of Inquisition into Heretical Depravity" (popularly known as the Inquisition), in 1233. The Inquisition entrusted emissaries—usually friars from mendicant orders such as the Dominicans and Franciscans—with the task of finding and eradicating heresy, especially in regions that had been rich in Cathar influence during the Albigensian Crusades. These inquisitors often worked in secret, making use of flimsy evidence, and were exempt from any authority save that which came from Rome. In 1252, not to be outdone by his predecessors in his zeal for orthodoxy, Pope Innocent IV (pope from 1243 to 54) empowered the Vatican's inquisitors to make use of torture to extract confessions.

One hundred years after its inception, the Inquisition rooted out what remained of Catharism, but as an engine of violence and repression, it was just getting started.[28] Although it was aimed first at Cathars and members of other splinter groups, the targets grew to include the Knights Templar; men and women suspected of sorcery, alchemy, and witchcraft; a wide assortment of renegade Catholics; and from the sixteenth century onward, Protestants.[29] In 1478, the Spanish Inquisition was established to prosecute Jewish converts to Christianity suspected of being less than sincere in their conversion.[30] The last victim of the Inquisition, a Spanish schoolteacher named Cayetano Ripoll, was put to death on July 26, 1826, and six hundred years of the Inquisition's ecclesiastically sanctioned bloodshed finally came to an end.[31]

Though the Catholic Church officially discontinued the practice of executing dissidents after Ripoll's death, a form of the Inquisition continues to this day, under a different name, as *Congregatio pro Doctrina Fidei*, Congregation for the Doctrine of the Faith. It no longer executes dissidents, but it does sometimes excommunicate or silence those Catholics whose work or theology is deemed heterodox. These include the leaders of the largest body of American nuns, whose faith was found lacking by the Congregation for the Doctrine of the Faith on April 18, 2012.[32] Between 1981 and 2005 the director of the Congregation for the Doctrine of the Faith was a German cardinal named Joseph Ratzinger. He left the position when he became Pope Benedict XVI.

CALVINIST VIOLENCE

It would be easy for me, as a Protestant and a Calvinist, to read the history of the Inquisition with the smugness of one whose spiritual heritage is free of bloodstains and smoke damage from the pyres of alleged heretics, but such pretense would be hypocrisy. The Reformation was violent from its beginnings. Martin Luther, the German reformer whose work in Wittenberg made him the father of Protestantism, was a virulent anti-Semite[33] who supported the suppression and slaughter of peasants who organized a revolt in an effort to reform the unjust system of medieval serfdom.[34] The story of England's transition to Protestantism is as blood-soaked as it is labyrinthine. Calvin's followers in France—known as the Huguenots—engaged in savage warfare with French Catholics throughout the latter half of the sixteenth century.[35]

Calvinists also tended to enforce orthodoxy by imitating the Roman Catholic Inquisition. I first heard of Calvinism's historical tendency to execute heretics when, in high school, I read Arthur Miller's *The Crucible.* The play retells the story of the infamous witch trials held in and around Salem, Massachusetts, in 1692 and 1693, trials carried out by Puritans against members of their own community. And there were even earlier Calvinist horrors back in Europe. While I was in college, I met my first Unitarians, a retired couple on a train between Oakland and Santa Barbara, California. The three of us were sharing four seats that faced each other, two on a side; somewhere near Salinas, they asked me about my religious convictions. When I told them I was a Presbyterian, they informed me that the founder of my tradition had killed the founder of their tradition back in the sixteenth century. I had no idea what they were talking about—apparently we didn't have a flannelgraph telling the story of John Calvin and Miguel de Servetus in my childhood Sunday school—so the Unitarians spent several hours telling me how my guy, John Calvin, had burned their guy, Servetus, at the stake.

It turns out the story of what transpired between Calvin and Servetus was more complicated—and in many ways, even more cruel—than the simple burning-at-the-stake described by my fellow travelers.

Miguel de Servetus was a brilliant man, a trained lawyer, theologian, and medical doctor who described the pulmonary circulation of blood in the human body some seventy-five years before an Englishman, William Harvey, was credited with the discovery. Though he had admirers and supporters, Servetus also happened to be Europe's most universally reviled heretic. By the time he was twenty, his writings denouncing the doctrine of the Trinity were circulating around Europe, causing scandal; Servetus spent most of his adult life living under an assumed name, practicing medicine but continuing to write tomes of heterodox theology.[36]

For years Calvin and Servetus carried on an extensive and increasingly acrimonious correspondence, which came to a close when an associate of Calvin's denounced Servetus to the Roman Catholic authorities in France, using letters and documents from the Calvin-Servetus correspondence. There is no question that Calvin himself provided this material;[37] some scholars believe that alerting the Inquisition to Servetus's whereabouts was Calvin's idea in the first place.[38]

Either way, French Catholic authorities arrested Servetus, but he escaped before he faced the Inquisition. Once on the lam he headed, for reasons that are not entirely clear, to Geneva, which happened to be the city where John Calvin lived and worked as the leader of the city's churches. Once in Geneva, Servetus went to hear Calvin preach. Someone recognized the brilliant heretic and directed the Genevan authorities to arrest him. That someone likely was Calvin himself.[39]

Servetus's trial was a matter of high drama, with political implications for Calvin and his standing in the city. With Calvin acting as lead witness for the prosecution, the heated exchanges that transpired during a protracted legal process were legendary as two of Europe's greatest minds met in a theological battle to the death.

Servetus lost the struggle and his life. The odds were against him. Not even Calvin's most vocal critics among Geneva's ruling elite (and there were many such vocal critics) had the political *cojones* to acquit so blatant a heretic as Miguel de Servetus. Through the whole process, Calvin's lone act of compassion (if you can call it that) was to beg the city magistrates to execute his old nemesis painlessly. The city fathers refused Calvin's entreaties, choosing instead to burn Servetus at the stake, a death made more painful by the fact that before Servetus (or since, for that matter), no one in Geneva ever had been burned at the stake. Servetus's executioners were inexperienced, and the pyre burned slowly. Miguel de Servetus died in unimaginable agony.[40]

THE PLIGHT OF THE ANABAPTISTS

The Servetus affair notwithstanding, Calvin and his followers in Geneva were among the least violent Protestants living in Europe during the sixteenth century. Yet far less violent than the Calvinists were the Anabaptists, who took Reformation-era ideas to an extreme. They rejected hierarchal church governance and embraced pacifism, refusing to participate in civil government and to take oaths. The Anabaptists' name is derived from the fact that they practiced adult—or believer's—baptism and re-baptized those who had received the sacrament of baptism as infants.[41]

The Anabaptist movement began in the Swiss city of Zurich, where the local Protestant city government (whose spiritual leader, Ulrich Zwingli, was an important voice in the Swiss-German Reformation), treated them harshly. According to Donald B. Kraybill and Carl Desportes Bowman, "Known as radical reformers, many Anabaptists paid dearly for tearing asunder the church-state fabric that had been woven together over the centuries. Thousands of Anabaptists were tortured and killed by religious and civil authorities—burned at the stake, drowned in lakes and rivers, starved in prisons, and beheaded by the sword."[42]

Ulrich Zwingli was not the only civil or ecclesiastical leader to persecute Anabaptists. Fleeing from the violence of fellow Protestant Christians, the Anabaptists became itinerant. In the end most of them fled Europe, choosing instead to live in the relative freedom afforded in North

America. Today we know them, among other names, as Mennonites, Amish, Brethren, Moravians, and Hutterites. As for Zwingli, though his legacy as an able theologian and an adept leader lives on, the leader of Zurich's reformation died a martyr's death, which from an Anabaptist's perspective may seem like just deserts. In 1531 Zwingli fought alongside the soldiers of Zurich in a religiously inspired war against a coalition of Swiss city-states who remained in communion with Rome. The enemies of Zurich and of the Reformation captured a badly wounded Zwingli. In short order they burned him at the stake and mixed his ashes with dung—a violent end for a Christian who, like many of his fellow reformers, lived by the sword.

MODERN PROTESTANT VIOLENCE

Although it would be tempting to say that the violence marking the sixteenth Christian century was a relic of the times—a result of internal struggle within the Christian family, and no longer present among Christians today—that would be wishful thinking. Christians remain violent.

In Northern Ireland and parts of Scotland, the sectarian rivalry between Catholics and Protestants often is palpable and sometimes erupts into armed conflict. Each year on the twelfth of July, members of Protestant fraternal organizations march through Roman Catholic neighborhoods in cities in Northern Ireland and Scotland, to assert and to celebrate the Protestant domination within the United Kingdom. July 12 is the anniversary of the Battle of Boyne in 1690, when Protestants loyal to William III (of Orange), king of England, Scotland (where he was William II), and Ireland (where he was known as King Billy) defeated the armies of the former King James II, William's Catholic uncle and father-in-law. Protestants organize the so-called Orange parades in part "to maintain intact the Protestant Constitution and Christian heritage of the United Kingdom."[43] However patriotic or benign the marchers' words may sound, the marching is an act of provocation that often turns nasty, as Roman Catholics respond by throwing rocks and Molotov cocktails.[44]

The tension between Catholics and Protestants in the British Isles is not limited to marching. In Scotland, games between Glasgow's two Premier League professional soccer teams, Celtic (a Catholic team) and Rangers[45] (Protestant), are cauldrons of ethnic pride, religious identity, and hooliganism. The shared vitriol has been so bad that the Scottish Parliament passed the Offensive Behaviour at Football and Threatening Communications (Scotland) Act 2012, a law that took effect on March 1, 2012. According to the Scottish government's Web site, the law "criminalizes behaviour which is threatening, hateful or otherwise offensive at a regulated [soccer] match including offensive singing or chanting." It applies "at, on the way to or from a 'regulated [soccer] match,' which includes league, European and international matches involving Scottish teams," and it carries a maximum penalty of five years in prison.[46]

When I was in Scotland three weeks after the law took effect, I wanted to watch the Rangers-Celtic game. However, I had a hard time finding a pub where my Scottish hosts felt I, as a Protestant clergyman who didn't hate Catholics, would be safe. In the week leading up to the game, I asked numerous soccer fans who self-identified as Rangers fans (and therefore as Protestants) to tell me what it meant to be a Protestant. Almost no one had any idea. Most people simply didn't possess the language with which to talk about religion in a way that was disassociated from soccer. This is, perhaps, religious violence at its most dangerous, when faith becomes tribal and hatred inspires activism that drifts into violence because it lacks a theological keel and moral compass.

WHY ARE CHRISTIANS VIOLENT?

I am a lifelong Christian who is conversant in the history of my faith, yet I have no idea why Christians are so violent. In places the Bible is a violent book, but contemporary American Christians seldom read the Bible's violent passages as normative; most Christians are far more conversant in the biblical language of peace and love and forgiveness than they are in the scriptural vocabulary of violence. Yet the history of the Christian church is often marked by violent beliefs and actions.

The preceding journey through eight hundred years of Christian violence is hardly exhaustive, focusing on violence that occurred among Roman Catholic and Protestant Christians living in Europe. Even within those relatively narrow confines, I have barely opened the cover of the book of Christian atrocities. Nonetheless, I have devoted the last several pages to a cursory look at Christian violence as a way of acknowledging the log in my Christian eye before turning my attention to the speck in the eyes of my Muslim sisters and brothers.

Although Islam over the years has not been as violent as Christianity, Islam's history, like Christianity's history, has been marked by a certain amount of violence. This violence should be addressed by any book attempting to discuss Islam.

If I cannot say for sure why Christian history is so violent, I can say even less about why the history of Islam also is marred by epochs and people who were—and in some cases, still are—hatefully bloodthirsty. I've read the Qur'an, and while it is not as violent as the Bible, some parts are disturbing. Scholars of Islam are quick to point out that the Qur'an, and indeed Islam itself, came into being in a violent time and place, and many of the more frightful passages found in the Qur'an speak directly to the conflicts that swirled around the Prophet and his followers at the birth of Islam.[47]

It is also true that Muslims—like most people who have amassed power and built empires through the years—used violence to keep power and hold territory. There is no evidence, however, that they were more violent than other peoples and governments who have built and sustained empires before and since. In fact, the armies of Islam were—in theory if not always in practice—guided by a set of rules for warfare that were extraordinary in their respect for human life and for their restraint on the field of battle.[48]

Of course, nothing from the history or theology of Islam can change the fact that on September 11, 2001, Muslim terrorists hijacked four airplanes and killed nearly three thousand innocent people. Nor can it change the fact that bloody acts of terror carried out in the name of Islam happen all over the world with alarming frequency.

In modern times a numerically small subset of Muslims has embraced violence and has made a habit of using terrorism—often cloaked in the guise of jihad—to further a political and religious agenda that isn't shared by most Muslims. The actions of this minority are as heinous as they are deadly, and the fact that they use religion to legitimize the abject sinfulness of terrorism compounds the ugliness of their actions.

MAINSTREAM ISLAM'S
CONDEMNATION OF VIOLENCE

Acts of terror notwithstanding, it would be impossible to overstate the extent to which religious violence lies outside the mainstream of Islam. When I was interviewing him for the second chapter of this book, I asked my friend Imam Tahir about violence in Islam. He said, "I was trained in a very traditional madrassa [Arabic for "school"], and way before 9/11 our teachers would tell us that even in places like Kashmir and Palestine, the struggle is not jihad, because going to war is no joke under Islamic law. There are too many requirements to make it work. Collateral damage, for example, is unavoidable in war, and it is not allowed under Islamic law. The rules, because they are so strict, guide us to make an amicable solution to our problems."

Tahir's observations are not unique to the kind of Muslim who lives in northern California. Muslims from all over the world and from every background insist that unprovoked violence is incompatible with Islam. A simple Google search using the words "Muslims condemn violence" will yield hundreds of formal Islamic declarations against violence in general and against terrorism in particular. In 2007 the Gallup organization surveyed residents of London and found that more Muslims (81 percent) felt violence is never justified than did their non-Muslim counterparts (72 percent).[49]

But the Gallup poll doesn't even do justice to how small the population of violent Muslims is (as distinct from those who may think violence sometimes is justified, but never actually engage in violence themselves). A better way to gauge the relatively insignificant size of violent populations is to look at numbers.

No one knows exactly how many Muslims there are in the world or how many of those are terrorists, but the best estimates put the world's Muslim population at between 1.5 and 1.6 billion souls. In 2009, the U.S. State Department estimated the membership in known Muslim terrorist organizations at somewhere between 18,000 and 36,000 individuals.[50] This means that one out of every 41,667 to 83,333 Muslims is a terrorist. The chances that a randomly selected Muslim will be a member of a known terrorist organization are slimmer than the odds of being dealt four of a kind in a hand of five-card poker from a fresh deck of well-shuffled cards; in fact, the odds that a randomly selected Muslim will be a terrorist are closer to the odds of being dealt a straight flush. This is to say it *could* happen that the Muslim sitting next to you on a flight from London to San Francisco is planning to carry out a dastardly plan involving explosives tucked into some unseen article of clothing, but the odds are extremely long.[51]

There is a greater likelihood that a randomly selected Muslim will be sympathetic with the goals and even the strategies of violent Muslims. The Pew Research Center found, for example, that a little more than half of all Jordanian Muslims had a favorable view of Osama bin Laden in May of 2003 (in secular Turkey, conversely, the late 9/11 mastermind's approval rating was at just 4 percent); the same study also found, however, that support for terror is determined more by political inclination than by religious affiliation.[52]

Though non-Muslims often call violent Muslims "fundamentalists," the brand of Islam that embraces the use of terror is a revolutionary form of Islam that has its roots in the nationalistic struggles that emerged after the breakup of the Ottoman Empire and the rise of Western colonialism, as well as in the emergence of modernism of the early to mid-twentieth century. The fact that the Muslims who embrace violence also happen to support regressive and oppressive social norms, especially with regard to the role of women in society, does not make them religious traditionalists. Like "fundamentalist" movements within Christianity and Judaism, theirs is a reactionary version of an ancient faith, one that hides modern innovation behind a veil of traditionalism.[53]

WHEN RELIGION BECOMES EVIL

The problem with quoting statistics about overall Muslim nonviolence is that it doesn't change the fact that even a small group of well-equipped, properly trained, and religiously motivated fanatics can cause serious damage. Nor do the statistics address the question of why some violent people use Islam to justify their actions.

Chances are that some Muslims are violent for the same reason that some Christians are violent: religion makes some people violent. In his book *When Religion Becomes Evil*, Charles Kimball, a scholar from Wake Forest University, suggests five warning signs that can lead to violence in religion. Religion becomes dangerous:

1. When religious people make absolute truth claims.
2. When a religious group requires blind obedience.

3. When a religious group claims to be ushering in an ideal or godly society.

4. When a religious group believes that its members' evil deeds are justified by the ideal world they are ushering in.

5. When religious groups feel empowered to declare holy war.[54]

Kimball's list of warning signs makes sense. These warning signs are found among a small minority of the adherents of nearly every tradition with which I am familiar.[55] Moreover, they can be found even among those whose "religion" is atheism; governments organized with atheism established as the officially sanctioned creed have demonstrated the capacity for ideologically inspired violence in the Stalinist purges, in Mao's Cultural Revolution, in the prisons of Cuba, and in the killing fields of Cambodia.

In the end, as I ponder the question of violence perpetrated in the name of God, as God is understood by people of every faith and no faith, I find myself returning to the Calvinist notion of human depravity: all of us are sinful, and some of us are evil. From time to time, the sin and evil that mark the human community are made worse by religion. It is the way of the world, but it is not the last word on the way of the world. Thankfully, most humans, though flawed, also are good, and most people are made better as they interact with the Divine. This is as true for Muslims as it is for Christians and anyone else who looks to heaven for solace and salvation.

Chapter 8

ISLAM AND WOMEN

Muhammad was one of those rare men who truly enjoy the company of women.

Karen Armstrong[1]

ONE OF THE MOST IMPORTANT, ENDURING, AND TIGHTLY HELD stereotypes of Islam involves the status of Muslim women. According to the dominant, non-Muslim narratives that tell the story of Muslim women, Islam is a misogynistic religion whose female adherents must wear burqas, cannot drive or get an education, and must stay at home behind the mud-wattle walls of the harems they share with their abusive husbands' several wives and multitudes of children. The script of this popular narrative goes on to say that women who opt out of the male-dominated expectations of the Muslim social norms—those who dare remain single, or who wear Western clothing, or who get an education and seek employment outside the home—will be shamed, shunned, and abused; some will be killed by jealous, chauvinistic male relatives.

This version of the life of Muslim women is perpetuated in the books and on the blogs of professional purveyors of Islamophobic propaganda—people such as Robert Spencer[2] and Pamela Geller[3]—but the narrative is found in more mainstream media as well. The August 9, 2010, cover of *Time* magazine, for example, published an image of an Afghan woman with a missing nose. The photograph illustrated the cover story, which warned against the potential dangers of a U.S. withdrawal from Afghanistan: without the benevolent protection of Western and Christian soldiers, we were told, the women of Afghanistan would be losing their noses and probably much worse.[4] One can read about the struggles of Muslim women in great works of literature such as Khaled Hosseini's novel *A Thousand Splendid Suns*,[5] which chronicles the difficult lives of Afghan women; in works of serious literary nonfiction such as *Nine Parts of Desire: The Hidden World of Islamic Women*,[6] in which Geraldine Brooks tells the stories of women she met while working as a Pulitzer Prize-winning Middle East correspondent for *The Wall Street Journal*; and in gripping first-person narratives written by Muslim women such as Irshad Manji, whose book *The Trouble with Islam Today: A Muslim's Call for Reform in Her Faith*[7] chronicles growing up among closed-minded Muslims in Canada, and Ayaan Hirsi Ali, a former member of the Dutch parliament, who has written the memoirs *Infidel*[8] and *Nomad*[9] to chronicle the struggles of women and girls in North Africa.

The idea that Muslim women suffer greater oppression than women of other faiths may, at first, seem to be self-evident to those unfamiliar with Islam, but as with every dominant narrative, it is worth asking if popularly held ideas about the oppression of Muslim women are true. Does being born into a Muslim family or society condemn women to a life of oppression, servitude, and suffering? The answer is complex and may present a bit of a surprise.

It would be naive at best and offensive at worst to suggest that women suffer no oppression or endure no abuse in many predominantly Muslim countries and communities, but the role of Islam in perpetuating the suffering of Muslim women should not be overstated, for suffering is not unique to Muslim women. Women suffer in every part of the world, and the suffering of Muslim women is not worse—and in some cases is not nearly as bad—as the suffering of women in non-Muslim societies.

HONOR KILLING AND FEMICIDE

Consider, for example, the crime of honor killing, in which men murder female relatives after finding out—or merely suspecting—that the victims have engaged in sexual relations without the permission of the men in their families. Sometimes this occurs even after the women or girls have been raped. It is a horrible and heinous crime, a form of femicide—the murder of a woman because she is a woman. What's worse, in those countries where honor killings occur, men who commit the murders seldom are brought to justice.

It is true that honor killing takes place in predominantly Muslim countries and in Muslim communities in Europe and North America. Yet in considering the role that Islam plays in promoting and condoning honor killings, it's worth noting that honor crimes and killings also take place among non-Muslim populations.

The United Nations estimates that some five thousand women are victims of honor crimes each year,[10] and Amnesty International has identified eighteen countries where honor crimes have been reported. Eight of the countries named by the Amnesty International report (Bangladesh, Egypt, Iran, Iraq, Jordan, Morocco, Pakistan, and Turkey) are predominantly Muslim; three (India, Israel, and Uganda) have large Muslim minority populations; and five (Canada, Italy, Sweden, the United Kingdom, and the United States) have significant Muslim communities. Two of the countries named by the report (Brazil and Ecuador) are predominantly Roman Catholic.[11]

That sixteen of the eighteen countries in which honor killings have been reported have significant Muslim populations seems like an indictment of Islam. But just because a country in which honor killings occur has a Muslim population, it does not necessarily follow that those honor killings occur exclusively among Muslims. Human Rights Watch, for example, has issued a report condemning honor killings in India's majority Hindu population,[12] and under Italian law, honor killing was considered justifiable homicide until 1981.[13]

It's also helpful to compare rates of honor killings in the Muslim world to rates of other forms of femicide. A report from an international conference on femicide held in 2008 revealed that in Jordan, a predominantly Muslim country, twenty women, on average, are murdered each year in honor killings.[14] The same document also reported that between 1993 and 2007, some thirty-five women, on average, were victims of femicide each year in the single Mexican city of Ciudad Juarez.[15] According to a study conducted by the University of California Hastings College of the Law in San Francisco, in Guatemala at least 375 women, on average, were victims of femicide each year between 2001 and 2005;[16] the Guatemala Human Rights Commission/USA reports 708 femicides in the Central American nation in 2009 and 630 in 2010.[17]

While Guatemala seems to be the country with the most femicides per annum overall, according to a Spanish study comparing the rates of femicide in Europe and the Americas, incidents of femicide in El Salvador are, per capita, proportionately higher even than in Guatemala. Turkey, the only predominantly Muslim country covered in the Spanish study, placed twenty-fourth out of forty-four countries.[18] From this we can see that non-Muslim countries can have tragically high rates of femicide: Mexico, El Salvador, and Guatemala, for example, are all predominantly Christian nations.

HUMAN TRAFFICKING

Like femicide, the trafficking of women and girls for sexual exploitation or for use as slave labor in homes and businesses is a global problem that receives scant attention. The United Nations describes human trafficking as a crime against humanity that "involves an act of recruiting, transporting, transfering, harbouring or receiving a person through a use of force, coercion or other means, for the purpose of exploiting them."[19] People of both sexes and of every age are victims of trafficking, but a disproportionate number of human trafficking victims are women and girls (according the United Nations, 66 percent of trafficking victims are women and 13 percent are girls).[20] An overwhelming majority of victims of human trafficking—79 percent, according to the United Nations[21]—are forced into sexual slavery. Human trafficking is a crime that causes unimaginable pain, and for the most part, it is committed with impunity.

The United States passed the William Wilberforce Trafficking Victims Protection Reauthorization Act of 2008. Besides strengthening American enforcement of antitrafficking laws, it directed the Secretary of State to compile a list of countries around the world whose laws and law-enforcement regimes are insufficient or ineffective in combating human trafficking.[22] When, in the following year, the State Department published a list of so-called third-tier countries[23]—those countries whose laws are not sufficient to combat human trafficking—Islam's detractors were quick to point out that nine of the seventeen third-tier countries were Muslim countries. This disproportionate representation of Muslim countries among those not doing enough to combat trafficking was, to some commentators, further evidence that Islam lacks a moral foundation.

"Actually, this is to be expected," wrote Robert Spencer in a blog entry titled "Breaking news! Muslim countries lead in human trafficking," "as slavery—whether infidels captured during the jihad, or whether one is born into it—is legitimate according to Islamic law."[24] In her blog *Atlas Shrugs*, Pamela Geller wrote, "The data in the report indicates that Muslim countries in the Middle East and Africa are continuing their centuries-old practice of human trafficking."[25]

But are these criticisms fair? With a few years now between us and the 2009 report, it's worth mentioning that the State Department's 2011 list of twenty third-tier countries (those that did not meet the United States' standards for fighting human trafficking) contained nine predominantly Muslim countries, nine predominantly Christian countries, and two communist countries.[26] If human trafficking has religious origins, blame certainly must be shared between two great religions and a system of belief that considers religion to be the opiate of the masses.

Whatever the prevailing religious proclivities in the nations that do not enforce laws against human trafficking, it is important to note that having insufficient laws and ineffective law enforcement is not the same as actually engaging in human trafficking. Because the trafficking of women and girls happens everywhere, there are many victims of trafficking in the Muslim world, but the countries in which women are at greatest risk are places where Christianity and Buddhism are the predominant religions. A study by the United Nations reports that

> in cases of human trafficking involving women and girls, "the main countries of origin are reported to be in Central and South-Eastern Europe, the Commonwealth of Independent States (CIS) and Asia, followed by West Africa, Latin America and the Caribbean. The most commonly reported countries of destination are in Western Europe, Asia and Northern America.[27]"

While the trafficking of women and girls is a global problem, predominantly Muslim regions of the world such as North Africa and the Middle East are notably absent from this list of places where such trafficking takes place. This does not exonerate those countries—Muslim or otherwise—that lack a legal and political will to combat human trafficking, but it does suggest that insofar as any religious tradition can be held responsible for the tragedy that is human trafficking, the sins of Islam do not seem to be worse than the sins of Buddhism and Christianity.

HEALTH CARE, EDUCATION, AND POVERTY

One measure of women's well-being is access to health care, and a good way of assessing the quality of health care available to women is to look at the rate of mortality in childbirth. On a list of maternal mortality compiled by *The Guardian* in 2010, the country with the highest rate of death in childbirth (1,575.1 deaths per 100,000 births) was Afghanistan, unquestionably a Muslim country (the country with the lowest rate of maternal mortality, by the way, was Italy, with 3.9 deaths per 100,000 births); but when it comes to maternal death rates, geography seems to matter more than religion. Among the forty most dangerous countries in which to give birth, twelve have a majority-Muslim population and thirty-six are in Africa. Among the forty nations with the lowest maternal mortality rates, three have Muslim-majority populations and thirty-one are in Europe and North America. For what it is worth, all of the Muslim countries that are among the forty safest nations in which to give birth have lower rates of maternal mortality than does the United States.[28]

Economics also plays a key role. On a list of countries broken down by the World Bank according to per capita purchasing power,[29] twenty-six of the world's poorest countries also are among the forty most dangerous countries in which to give birth. Of the twenty-six countries that are both among the poorest and among the most prone to maternal mortality, eight are predominantly Muslim. These numbers suggest that when it comes to maternal health, economics is far more influential than is religion.

In their book *Half the Sky*, Nicholas Kristof and Sheryl WuDunn suggest four factors that contribute to maternal mortality. The first is biology. Because humans have relatively small pelvises and large heads, we are the only mammals that require assistance while giving birth. When that assistance isn't available, women are more prone to die during childbirth. The second factor is education. When women are educated, birthrates fall, thereby diminishing the chances a woman will suffer during labor and delivery. The third factor is a lack of rural health services. In many poor countries, there aren't enough doctors and clinics in rural areas, which often are home to the poorest populations. The fourth factor that contributes to maternal mortality is a disregard for women. In many societies, the health and well-being of women isn't considered to be as important as the health and well-being of men. As an epigraph to the seventh chapter of their book, Kristof and WuDunn quote a rhetorical question posed by Asha-Rose Migiro, the United Nations' Deputy Secretary General, who asked, "Would the world stand by if it were men who were dying just for completing their reproductive function?"[30]

Looking at the list of factors compiled by Kristof and WuDunn, it's hard to single out Islam as being uniquely responsible for maternal mortality in developing countries. Certainly Islam is not responsible for how humans have evolved, nor can it be blamed for a lack of medical care in rural communities.

The idea that Islam discourages its female adherents from being educated certainly is put forward by Islam's many detractors,[31] but the data don't necessarily support that conclusion. When comparing rates of women's literacy (and therefore, access to education) around the world,[32] it's true that the country where women are least literate is Afghanistan, and that twenty-one of the forty countries with the lowest rate of female literacy are countries with Muslim majorities. (By comparison, eleven of the forty countries with the lowest levels of female literacy are Christian, five practice traditional religions, two are Buddhist, and one is Hindu.) Meanwhile, only three of the forty countries with the highest rates of women's literacy are Muslim-majority countries. (By comparison, thirty-four of the countries with the highest female literacy are traditionally Christian, one is officially atheist, one is predominantly Buddhist, and one has a majority Shinto population.) At first, this can seem like an indictment of Islam, yet all but ten of the forty countries with the lowest rates of women's literacy are in Africa, while all but ten of the countries with the highest rates of women's literacy are in Europe. It is entirely possible that when it comes to women's access to education, region trumps religion. As with maternal mortality, economics may also play a role in determining whether or not women and girls will become educated. Thus twenty-five of the world's poorest forty nations (eight of which are Muslim) also are among the forty countries with the least literate female populations. Poverty seems to be an important a factor when determining what prevents women and girls from learning to read.

The idea that Islam holds women in low esteem and could, therefore, play a role in global rates of maternal mortality, is addressed by Kristof and WuDunn in *Half the Sky*.[33] Their conclusion—that many Muslim societies are misogynistic even if Islam itself isn't necessarily misogynistic—is reasonable enough, but their decision to explore Islam and misogyny struck me as odd. In *Half the Sky* an analysis of Islam's attitudes toward women comes directly after three chapters dedicated to maternal mortality. In those chapters the authors describe deplorable conditions for childbirth in Ethiopia and Cameroon—both of which are predominantly Christian countries—and they expose the detriment to women's health that has resulted from American Evangelical activists' pressuring the United States government to defund United Nations programs that support women's reproductive health in the developing world. Given this context, one might wonder why the authors didn't write a chapter asking if Christianity is misogynist.

The bottom line is that twenty-eight of the forty most dangerous countries in which to give birth are not Muslim countries. And nineteen of the countries with the lowest rates of female literacy are not Muslim countries. The countries where childbirth is most dangerous and where female illiteracy is most prevalent have two things in common: they are overwhelmingly poor and African. Of the world's forty poorest countries, thirty-seven are either among the countries with the highest levels of maternal fatality or among the forty countries with the lowest rates of female literacy. Regardless of the degree to which some Muslim societies disregard the well-being of women, the numbers seem to indicate that Islam does not have a monopoly on the kind of misogyny that prevents women from enjoying the benefits of health care and education.

Those who wish to improve the lot of the world's women should not focus on Islam, but should start by supporting economic development for women, especially in Africa.

POLITICAL EMPOWERMENT

But even when they can read and have access to medicine, are Muslim women not politically disenfranchised? It is true that many women in Muslim countries suffer political and economic marginalization—in Saudi Arabia, for example, women remain unable to vote—but it is also true that Pakistan, one of the world's largest Muslim countries, had a female prime minister in 1988, two years before women in the Roman Catholic Swiss canton of Appenzell Innerrhoden won the right to vote in local elections.[34]

Another important measure of women's political involvement is the number of women serving in national legislative bodies. A survey by the International Parliamentary Union ranked the world's countries based on the percentage of women serving in national legislative bodies. While it is true that two predominantly Muslim countries—Saudi Arabia and Qatar—joined the Democratic Republic of the Congo, the Solomon Islands, Palau, Nauru, Micronesia, and Belize for dead last, having no women legislators, it is also true that the United States tied with Turkmenistan for seventy-eighth place, behind the following predominantly Muslim countries: Morocco, the United Arab Emirates, Kazakhstan, Indonesia, Tajikistan, Bangladesh, Uzbekistan, Mauritania, Pakistan, Senegal, Kyrgyzstan, Sudan, Iraq, Afghanistan, and Burundi.

In fact, it's hard to find a category of women's suffering in which women in predominantly Muslim countries suffer worse than their counterparts living in the areas of Africa, Latin America, and Southeast Asia, all places where Islam is not the major religion. Driving is one such category—as of this writing, Saudi Arabia remains the only country in which women are not allowed to drive. Other than that, the disempowerment of women seems to exist equally in different religious contexts. Comparing facts and statistics from around the world does not exonerate the mistreatment of women when it occurs in the Muslim world, nor does it alleviate anyone's suffering. It does, however, suggest that when Muslim women suffer from violence and abuse, it may have less to do with the religious affiliation of the perpetrators of that violence and more to do with their misogyny.

WOMEN IN THE QUR'AN

If the data disprove the dominant narrative that portrays Islam as a singularly misogynistic faith, it should come as no surprise to anyone who has read the Bible and the Qur'an side by side, looking for ways the sacred texts of Christianity and Islam portray women. The Qur'an uses some variation of the word "woman" in 177 different places.[35] For the most part, when the Qur'an speaks of women, it does so in the context of marriage and domestic life. In this way the Qur'an reads very much like the laws of Moses: as with the Bible, in the Qur'an, it seems—to a first-time reader anyway—that women are meant to be subservient to men. This is consistent with the fact that the Qur'an is more than 1,300 years old.

Like the Bible, the Qur'an celebrates faithful women such as Hagar, the mother of Ishmael, and Mary, the mother of Jesus. Like the Bible, the Qur'an contains passages that have the potential to make a modern reader uncomfortable. For example, the Qur'an requires that a woman or girl's inheritance should be half of what a brother might inherit,[36] and it requires two women to testify on a matter in which a single man would suffice.[37] Like the Bible, the Qur'an permits polygamy,[38] and like the Bible, sex during menstruation is forbidden.[39] As with the Bible, the Qur'an directs women to dress modestly,[40] and while the particulars around what that modest dress should look like varies from Muslim to Muslim, some devout Muslim women will cover every part of their bodies except for their hands and face (though some Muslim women cover their hands and faces as well). It's probably worth pointing out that Islam's rules for modesty require men to be similarly modest. Though the head covering isn't as complete for devout men as it is for devout women, according to some Muslim traditions men must cover every part of their bodies save their hands (up to the wrist) and their heads, though a head covering often is worn as well.[41]

Unlike the Bible, the Qur'an does not blame Eve for humanity's fall from grace, as does the New Testament (1 Timothy 2:14, interpreting Genesis 3). Nor does the Qur'an require a raped woman to marry her attacker, as does the Bible in Deuteronomy 22:28. The Qur'an does not suggest childbirth as a pathway to salvation, as does the Bible in 1 Timothy 2:15. It is beyond the purview of this chapter to catalog all of the biblical passages betraying misogyny that surpasses anything found in the Qur'an, yet it is worth acknowledging that any Christian who wishes to criticize the treatment of women in the Qur'an should do so with an appreciation for irony.

INGRID MATTSON

Just as many Christian women lead happy, productive, and deeply spiritual lives despite the Bible's considerable misogyny, it is honest to acknowledge that despite the Qur'an's relatively mild misogyny, many Muslim women are educated and successful, exercising leadership in politics, business, academics, and in a wide variety of professions. One such woman is Ingrid Mattson, a Canadian-born religious scholar who, despite her Muslim faith, teaches in the religion department at the historically Anglican Huron University College in London, Ontario. In 2006, Dr. Mattson was elected president of the Islamic Society of North America (ISNA), a post she held for four years. Professor Mattson was the first woman and the first convert to serve as the head of North America's largest Muslim organization.

I caught up with Professor Mattson via Skype. It was during Ramadan, and as we talked, we were joined by her dog, Iggy, who appeared to be a German Shepherd mix and was full of energy. "During Ramadan, he doesn't get as much exercise as he is used to," she told me apologetically. Iggy brought her an empty water bottle. Dr. Mattson threw it off screen somewhere, and I could hear Iggy scurrying after it and then gnawing on the plastic. I asked Professor Mattson what it was like to be a woman who is a leader in the Muslim world, both as an advocate and as a scholar of international reputation.

She tossed the bottle for Iggy once more and told me of the respect and honor she receives because she is a scholar and a leader. That she is a woman seems to matter less than even she expected, even among more traditionalist Muslims in North America. As president of ISNA, Dr. Mattson received and accepted many invitations to speak in front of Muslim organizations, and she was always well received, even when she addressed conservative groups.

The warmth and respect she received in North America were extended overseas as well. "I did have a question about what would happen internationally," she told me, "and it has been remarkable. I have never experienced anything but respect and support from scholars all over the world. When I went to international conferences, the people were polite and nice, and once we started to do real scholarly work, I saw that they weren't just being polite and nice, but they were appreciating my contributions."

Dr. Mattson went on to tell me about her scholarly interactions with Muslim academics from around the world—even from more traditional countries such as Yemen, Egypt, and Saudi Arabia. "In the Muslim world there's an appreciation of competence," she told me, "and they honor what they perceive to be a desire on my part to serve and to help benefit the Muslim community."

This is not to say that every Muslim scholar has received Dr. Mattson as an equal, but for the most part, she has found a lack of acceptance only among a small number of conservative scholars, most of whom live and work in Saudi Arabia. Elsewhere, even among scholars who might not want to have women in their own families being active like Dr. Mattson, she is accepted and respected.

But even Saudi Arabia, which is home to some of Islam's most conservative scholars, has not been a place of total rejection for Dr. Mattson. "It's remarkable," she told me, "when I was in Saudi Arabia for hajj, I was accepted and respected as a scholar. My hajj tour leader was a scholar at the university in Riyadh, and he was very conservative. As it happened, I had the best Arabic in the group, so I got to be the translator, and by the end of the tour, this scholar wanted me to come and present a paper in Medina at a conference they were having. It was interesting watching this man's transformation. He was always friendly, but at first he was just friendly. By the end of the hajj, he was speaking to me as a peer. A lot of people in the Muslim world just haven't had the opportunity to meet and to know a woman who is a scholar."

My impression of Ingrid Mattson is that she is someone who has embraced Islam without adopting the unquestioning dogmatic zeal common among converts of every kind. Because she seemed so comfortable with change, I asked Dr. Mattson what changes she felt were needed and necessary for the well-being of women in the Muslim world.

"It differs from place to place," she told me, "but the most important thing that has to change is that women need to be included in all levels of governance. That means they need to be on the board of the local mosque, and they need to be in municipal, regional, and national governments." Dr. Mattson has seen this need for greater representation in decision-making bodies everywhere from refugee camps in Afghanistan to middle-class mosques in the United States. The problem, she told me, is the paternalism that is pervasive in traditional Muslim societies. Men—with the best of intentions—think they know what is best for women, even though it never occurs to them that they might seek out a woman's opinion before making decisions that affect the female members of the community.

"The men sit together on their boards or in their committee meetings, and they might come up with what they think is a good design for their new mosque, for example; and the men who designed it thought they'd done everything right, but it's only after construction is started and the women see it and they say 'Hey, wait a minute—we need a family room or a crying-baby room, or have you noticed that the women's space is lacking in basic amenities?' This is the real issue. The mosque issue is just a small example of what happens all the time at a larger level. We need to get away from the belief that some people can represent the entire community. We need to be aware of the problems with the lack of representation."

I asked her how she thought the condition of Muslim women is trending—if she thought things were getting better or worse. She told me that for women the future looks mixed. Women are becoming better educated, and in the process are learning more about the important role of women in the history of Islam and about the ways Islam can empower women. Women are having more discussions on controversial topics and are engaging in more serious scholarship. Much of the improvement in women's education has come as a result of technology, which has enabled the formation of a global and cosmopolitan Muslim community not seen since European colonialism broke up the Muslim empires and their networks of Arabic-speaking scholarly communities. This new international virtual community of scholarship has provided a forum for interesting and empowering conversations around women's issues.

"On the other hand," Dr. Mattson told me, "in many parts of the Muslim world, things remain bad for women and are even getting worse." She pointed out that the majority of Muslims (and therefore the majority of Muslim women) live in poor countries with autocratic, or at least nondemocratic, governments. They face the same challenges and hardships that women face in every country that is poor and governed by autocratic regimes. "Wherever there is military and political insecurity," she reminded me, "or when there is poverty and corruption, women tend to suffer more than men. So when we look across the Muslim world, we see a lot of poverty and warfare, and so of course women suffer. Women suffer because women are susceptible to sexual violence during times of war. As a result, they tend to stay home. They stop going to school and to work. This was something that was really problematic during the invasion of Iraq, and it remains a problem in Afghanistan. Most non-Muslims interpret the struggles of women as stemming from a religious cause, but that's really much too simplistic."

HOW MY MIND HAS CHANGED

I was glad for my conversation with Ingrid Mattson because it helped to confirm a change in my own attitudes and beliefs that occurred over the course of writing this book. As it happens, the first thing I did after deciding to write this book was read a collection of books on Islam that had gathered in my library over the years. I read them in no particular order. I just started taking them off the shelf randomly, the first being the above-mentioned *Nine Parts of Desire: The Hidden World of Islamic Women*, by Geraldine Brooks. It is not a book that flatters Islam, but it's convincingly written; its portrayal of Muslim women fits nicely alongside images and ideas I'd gleaned from the masterful novels of Khaled Hosseini, and from the broader culture in which I am steeped.

At the beginning of this project, I didn't question the dominant narratives surrounding the well-being (or lack thereof) of Muslim women. As I worked on this book, however, I began to suspect that my ideas—and indeed, the dominant narratives about Muslim women—were too simplistic. As I spoke with Muslim women—especially Maha ElGenaidi (see chap. 10) and Ingrid Mattson—and as I asked the questions necessary to challenge common ideas about Islam and women, it became apparent to me that when it comes to the well-being of women, Islam and Christianity have a lot in common.

One could assess the condition of Christian women by looking at powerful women in America who self-identify as Christians: politicians from Hillary Clinton to Condoleezza Rice, writers from Flannery O'Connor to Anne Lamott, and countless intellectuals, pastors, business and community leaders, teachers, and artists. If you look at Christendom from the right perspective, it looks as if Christian women are doing just fine.

On the other hand, when I leave my house in the predominantly Hispanic Mayfair district of East San José and walk to the café where I write in San José's Little Portugal, I pass a small Spanish-language church—La Luz del Mundo (the Light of the World)—that requires women to cover their heads with black lace mantillas. It is but one of several such churches in my neighborhood. In fact, head coverings are common in several Christian traditions, including conservative strands of Catholicism (in churches where the Latin Mass is used) and in the more traditional Anabaptist churches, such as the Old Order Mennonites and the Amish. Sometimes Christian women and girls who cover their heads also must wear clothing that is cumbersome, awkward, and that restricts the kinds of activities they can do.

But limited wardrobe choices may be the least of the problems that Christian women face. In the United States a growing number of Protestant Evangelicals subscribe to the "Quiver-full" movement, which requires women to bear as many children as possible.[42] Opposition to state-mandated programs that would vaccinate girls against the human papillomavirus (HPV), a leading cause of cervical cancer, has occurred among some American Christians, many of whom worship in churches that require women to remain silent and that prohibit them from holding positions of leadership. (It's telling that Texas Governor Rick Perry's once-promising campaign for the Republican presidential nomination unraveled after fellow conservatives attacked him for supporting an HPV vaccination program in Texas,[43] a program opposed by the influential Evangelical magazine *Christianity Today*).[44] And for American Christian women, life is good when compared to the lives that many women live in some majority-Christian nations of Latin America, where as we've already seen, femicide rates are among the highest in the world, or in the Christian parts of Africa, where access to health care and education is limited, at best.

So it is with women in Islam. It's possible to look at the lives women lead in the Muslim world and see progress and empowerment, and it is possible to see suffering and oppression. As with Christianity, both perspectives are valid, but for those of us who are concerned about the health and well-being of women, the most important work is not changing Christianity or Islam. Rather, the more urgent need is to change societies and the men who dominate them so that women can pursue lives that are healthy, productive, and free.

Part 5

The American Cult of Fear

Basics: What Are the Five Pillars?

A few weeks after the terrorist attacks of September 11, 2001, a local Muslim community association opened the doors of its mosque and elementary school, inviting non-Muslims to learn about Islam. The event was overwhelmingly successful. More than a thousand people crowded into the mosque's main prayer space, which was designed to hold maybe five hundred. I arrived on time, which turned out to be a bit late, but in an effort to demonstrate interfaith goodwill, I wore a clerical collar, and my status as a Christian clergyman earned me a place of honor. Ushers whisked me to the front of the crowd, where no seats remained, but I found a good place on the floor. From my place up front, I had a good view of a group of kindergarteners who stood in front of the gathered crowd and sang, to the tune of *Frère Jacques*, the following song:

What is Islam? What is Islam?
Don't you know? Don't you know?
It is five pillars. It is five pillars.
Now you know. Now you know.

But, of course, I didn't yet know what the five pillars were, so children from each of the school's five grades above kindergarten stood up to present the five pillars of Islam.

The first pillar of Islam is its *core statement of belief:* "There is no God but God, and Muhammad is the messenger of God." To be authentic, this statement of faith really should be said in Arabic (*'ilāha 'illà l-Lāh, Muḥammadun rasūlu l-Lāh*), and in that mosque overflowing with visitors, first graders dressed in outfits from around the Muslim world proclaimed the faith of their parents in hesitant Arabic, many of them lisping for want of front teeth.

Then the second graders stood up to present Islam's second pillar, which is *ritual prayer.* Muslims are encouraged to pray at all times in any language that feels comfortable to them, but five times a day—at daybreak, noon, late afternoon, sunset, and nightfall—they join together in a standardized Arabic prayer that involves a set script and a choreographed series of bows and prostrations. A precocious second grader called his classmates to prayer, using the traditional and universal invitation:

God is most great. God is most great.
God is most great. God is most great.
I testify that there is no god except God.
I testify that there is no god except God.
I testify that Muhammad is the messenger of God.

I testify that Muhammad is the messenger of God.
Come to prayer! Come to prayer!
Come to success [in this life and the Hereafter]!
Come to success!
God is most great. God is most great.
There is no god except God.

The rest of the class then demonstrated the motions of prayer, standing shoulder to shoulder, facing Mecca.

The third pillar of Islam is *charity*. Muslims are required each year to give 2.5 percent of their net worth to those in need. The third graders performed a skit demonstrating the pillar of generosity in which a girl looked at her wallet after receiving gifts on her birthday. After kind words from her mother, she ended up giving a dollar to a fund that helped orphans in Malaysia.

Prior to the big event, the fourth-grade class had held a contest to see who could write the best essay about *Ramadan*, the fourth pillar of Islam, and the virtue of fasting. Ramadan is the ninth month in the Islamic calendar, which is lunar, meaning that from the perspective of those using a solar calendar, it is a movable month, cycling through the Western calendar every thirty-four years. Ramadan was a month in the Arab calendar before the rise of Islam, but it was set aside as special for Muslims because Muhammad received his first revelations of the Qur'an during the month of Ramadan. Ever since, Muslims have abstained from eating, drinking, and having sex between sunup and sundown during Ramadan. It is a time of prayer, spiritual renewal, and charity. It is also a time of celebration with family, friends, and community, as the breaking of each daily fast becomes a joyful feast.

Three fourth graders read their winning essays about Ramadan, each written with a longing to participate in the fast, something that was still a few years off for the nine-year-old essayists. Prepubescent children don't fast during Ramadan, nor do pregnant women, nursing mothers, or anyone else whose health would be harmed by a lack of nutrients and hydration.

The fifth and final pillar is *the hajj*, or the pilgrimage to Mecca. It is obligatory for all Muslims who are able, financially and physically, to travel at least once to Islam's holiest city during the twelfth month of the Arab calendar. The fifth graders presented a multimedia description of what happens on the hajj. Pilgrims wear identical white garments, which symbolize the equality of all Muslims, and they perform a variety of sacred acts, including walking around the cube-shaped Kaaba and running seven times across a stretch of desert in memory of Hagar, who, according to tradition, came to the same place looking for water. Pilgrims throw stones at a rock that represents the devil, and they pray together in the desert, asking for God's forgiveness.

For Muslims, as the name implies, the five pillars provide structure to the life of faith. They are joyful obligations meant to point faithful Muslims toward God and to deepen their experience of the divine. In some ways, the song of the kindergarteners was not entirely correct: Islam is more than the five pillars, but to the extent that Islam would not exist in its current form without the pillars, the children's song was true.

Chapter 9

OBSESSION VERSUS *JESUS CAMP*

O you who believe, you shall reverence GOD, and be among the truthful.

Qur'an 9:119

You shall not bear false witness against your neighbor.

Exodus 20:16

ARE MUSLIMS NAZIS?

This, at first, may seem like a ridiculous question that calls to mind absurd images of Adolf Hitler and Eva Braun inviting Malcolm X and Betty Shabazz over for dinner at the Berghoff. Yet despite the cognitive dissonance inherent in the suggestion that Islam—even in its most radicalized and militant iterations—is a latter-day manifestation of the political philosophy espoused by Francisco Franco in Spain, Benito Mussolini in Italy, and Adolf Hitler in Germany, many Americans are convinced that contemporary Islam is a reincarnation of fascism.

For example, it is common for writers critical of Islam to use the term "Islamofascist" to describe Islamic ideologies that oppose American hegemony. According to William Safire, a proponent of the term, "Islamofascism" first was used in 1990 to describe radical Muslims, but it came into popular use after 2001, thanks in large part to atheist critics of Islam such as Christopher Hitchens.[1]

Islam, of course, is a religion whose adherents come from every nook and cranny of human existence; fascism is, according to *Merriam-Webster's Collegiate Dictionary*, "a political philosophy, movement, or regime (as that of the *Fascisti*) that exalts nation and often race above the individual and that stands for a centralized autocratic government headed by a dictatorial leader, severe economic and social regimentation, and forcible suppression of opposition."[2] Although Islam and fascism hardly click together with Lego-like ease, the perception of a connection exists.

OBSESSION

The conflation of Islam and fascism received perhaps its biggest boost in September of 2008. A little-known organization called The Clarion Fund, in an apparent attempt to bolster the presidential aspirations of John McCain, distributed 28 million copies of a 2006 film called *Obsession: Radical Islam's War against the West*, mostly via compact discs inserted as advertisement supplements in daily newspapers in swing states.[3]

It's a creepy film. *Obsession* begins like a minimalist experiment. The screen is black, and the deep, electronic droning of an 1980s-era synthesizer sets an ominous vibe. It's very "Mark Rothko-meets-Philip Glass." White letters appear on the black screen, spelling out Edmund Burke's famous maxim, "The only thing necessary for evil to triumph is for good men to do nothing."

The musical tone shifts slightly as the Irish philosopher's words fade away, while an image of a gunman emerges, presumably a militant member of Hamas. His face is masked by a Palestinian kaffiyeh (a traditional head covering that also can be used as a scarf), and his assault rifle points straight at the viewer. The white letters return, this time with a disclaimer: "This film is about Islamic extremism, a dangerous ideology fueled by misled religious hatred."

The synthesizer adds another layer of tonality to the droning musical score as the image of a gunman dissolves, while a man in Muslim-looking garb[4] emerges on the screen. He is holding aloft a photo of Osama bin Laden. Then we see a man yelling, his fist lashing in orbit above his head. Next comes an image of a mass rally in Iran.

The Rothko-Glass vibe returns, and after a few seconds so do white-lettered words: "It is important to remember, most Muslims are peaceful and do not support terror." The words fade away, and we see friendly images: two women pushing a stroller, some guys riding in a horse-drawn carriage, and a pair of university students walking and laughing together. Then more words appear: "This film is not about them."

Suddenly a drumbeat is added to the multilayered synthesizer drone. It feels almost like technodance music, only ominous. Images of Hezbollah fighters show up on the screen. After a few seconds they are gone, and the screen is black again. More words: "This film is about a radical worldview and the threat it poses to us all, Muslim and non-Muslim alike." The screen is filled with images of Palestinian youths dancing around a burning American flag. Above the droning synthesizers and the beating drums, a wailing voice sings what sounds like a Middle-Eastern melody. The film's opening credits begin to roll.

The opening credits say a lot about *Obsession*. The first name listed, that of executive producer Peter Mier, is a pseudonym. In fact, according to an article in the Israeli newspaper *Haaretz*, only the producer, Raphael Shore, and its director-editor, Wayne Kopping, used their real names in association with the film. The rest of film's production staff preferred to remain anonymous.[5] Apparently the film-makers were afraid of being treated like Salman Rushdie for their participation in the making of *Obsession*.

The secrecy that shrouds the film extends not just to the filmmakers but also to those who funded the project. The Clarion Fund, which financed and distributed the film, describes itself as

> a non-profit organization that aims to educate Americans about issues of national security. The organization focuses primarily on the urgent and growing threat of Radical Islam. To that end, Clarion produces and distributes documentary films and facilitates online education and outreach to help Americans better understand the real dangers posed by radical Islam while exposing a side of the story that is often overlooked or misrepresented by the media.

The Clarion Fund began its existence in 2006 with the initial release[6] of *Obsession*, and about the only thing known about the organization—other than its role in the production and distribution of *Obsession* and another film called *The Third Jihad* (which we will examine in the next chapter)—is that it is connected to Aish HaTorah (Hebrew for "Fire of the Torah"), an Israeli educational organization.

The connection is loose: the Clarion Fund shares a mailing address with the offices of Aish HaTorah's American fund-raising arm, and a few of Clarion's board members and employees have worked for Aish HaTorah. For its part, Aish HaTorah denies any involvement in the film or its distribution.[7]

Regardless of affiliation and funding, the mostly anonymous makers of *Obsession* seem to have been single-minded in the goal of using sixty minutes to make Islam seem as nefarious as possible and Muslims as suspect as possible. After the opening credits, the film starts with the attacks of Tuesday, September 11, 2001, and then remembers a terrorist attack for various days of the week, including Madrid and London (each on a Thursday: Madrid, March 11, 2004; London, July 7, 2005); and Beslan, Chechnya (on Friday, September 17, 2004). Terrorist attacks in Bali and Istanbul also receive mention. Illustrating each event are grisly images of violent death, interspersed with shots of radical Muslims chanting, "Death to America!" The music grows in intensity.

Following the roll call of terrorism, the film features the views and opinions of various commentators, each portraying Islam in a negative light. The commentaries are interspersed with disturbing images of militants and victims of terror. Everything seems orchestrated to betray the film's initial promise: "This film is about Islamic extremism, a dangerous ideology fueled by misled religious hatred. It is important to remember, most Muslims are peaceful and do not support terror. This film is not about them."

About halfway through the film, a voice of sanity and hope emerges. Khaleel Mohammed, a Muslim scholar at San Diego State University (who later apologized for his role in the film),[8] informs the viewer that the word "jihad," which until now has been used as a synonym for "holy war," actually refers primarily to an inner struggle. It is a short moment of nuance and balance that is cut short—interrupted, almost—when the film cuts to Walid Shoebat, one of *Obsession*'s most prominent commentators, whom the film identifies as a former PLO terrorist. "'Jihad' does mean self-struggle," acknowledges Shoebat, "but so does 'Mein Kampf.'"

Then things get really strange.

Suddenly *Obsession* is no longer a simple critique of Islam; its portrayal of Muslims no longer can be contained by such adjectives as "violent," "extremist," and "anti-American." During the film's second half, *Obsession* makes a startling claim: Muslims are Nazis.

The filmmakers' connection between Islam and Nazism is based on the following commonalities (most of which are, at best, debatable). First, some Muslims, like all Nazis, are anti-Semites. Second, some Muslims are trying to take over the world, just like the Third Reich. Third, the Palestinian Mufti of Jerusalem was an ally of Hitler. Fourth, not everyone in the United States and the United Kingdom believes Islam is a threat, just as not everyone believed that Germany, under the leadership of Hitler, was capable of the horrors that marked World War II. The considerable differences between Nazism and Islam are ignored in *Obsession*, however. These differences include (but certainly are not limited to) the fact that Islam is a racially inclusive ancient religious tradition and Nazism was a brief, profoundly racist expression of fascist political ideology, which, though it still has some adherents, failed to outlive the Second World War.

It is an interesting rhetorical sleight of hand: present a few similarities—either real or fabricated—but ignore important differences, and the unsuspecting viewer is left to assume a connection where none exists. Using the logic of *Obsession*, one could suggest that the Amish are really Ultra-orthodox Jews: members of both groups wear old-fashioned clothing, women from both groups cover their heads, men from both groups grow beards, and members of both groups speak languages derived from German (Pennsylvania Dutch and Yiddish).

Obsession has other problems. For example, the film has an odd tendency to show Iranian protestors while speaking about Arab Muslims, despite the fact that Iranians are not Arabs and that Iranians almost always are Shiites, while most Arabs are Sunni Muslims. This lack of precision may reflect the fact that among the seventeen "experts" interviewed for the film, only one—the above-mentioned Khaleel Mohammed—is a scholar of Islam, and his only inclusion in the film seems to be used as a setup.

The fact that the filmmakers present the above-mentioned Walid Shoebat as an expert on Islam is typical of the film's imprecision, raising questions about *Obsession's* credibility. Now an Evangelical Christian, Walid Shoebat's reputation is not without blemish. Chris Hedges, the Pulitzer Prize-winning former Middle East bureau chief for *The New York Times*, has described Shoebat as a "stooge of the Christian Right," "a fraud," and a "con artist."[9] It's certainly clear that *Obsession* presents Mr. Shoebat as an expert on radical Islam because he was once a member of the Palestinian Liberation Organization (PLO). My objection to this qualification is that the PLO is a secular organization with no formal connection to religious extremism. Again, *Obsession*'s filmmakers were not obsessed with detail. The "experts" interviewed for *Obsession* include a long list of ex-Muslims, journalists, filmmakers, activists, political scientists, lawyers, historians, a former spy, and even an erstwhile member of the Hitler Youth.

Now, journalists, political scientists, lawyers, and activists often are well-read, intelligent people, but it is telling that the filmmakers were either unwilling or unable to track down an actual scholar of Islam willing to support the film's central thesis, that Islam is a latter-day incarnation of Nazi-like fascism.

WELCOME TO JESUS CAMP

Despite its failings, *Obsession* is slick; and film, particularly documentary film, is a powerful medium. It's hard not to believe what one sees on a screen of any size. After all, images must exist in order to be captured through a lens. The problem with lenses, however, is that in order to capture an image, they must necessarily ignore the images and ideas that frame the shot. The problem with *Obsession* lies less in what it says than in what it does not say. By focusing only on extremely negative images of Islam (some of them fictitious) and ignoring what is good in Islam, *Obsession* presents a distorted picture.

A similar critique can be made of the film *Jesus Camp*, a documentary by filmmakers Heidi Ewing and Rachael Grady. Any Christian wondering how a Muslim may feel while watching *Obsession* should watch *Jesus Camp* and imagine someone presenting *Jesus Camp* in the Muslim world as a fair and balanced representation of Christianity.

Jesus Camp's Web site introduces the film in the following way:

> A growing number of Evangelical Christians believe there is a revival underway in America that requires Christian youth to assume leadership roles in advocating the causes of their religious movement. Jesus Camp . . . follows Levi, Rachael, and Tory to Pastor Becky Fischer's "Kids on Fire" summer camp in Devil's Lake, North Dakota, where kids as young as six years old are taught to become dedicated Christian soldiers in "God's army." The film follows these children at camp as they hone their "prophetic gifts" and are schooled in how to "take back America for Christ." The film is a first-ever look into an intense training ground that recruits born-again Christian children to become an active part of America's political future.[10]

The filmmakers have taken pains to say that *Jesus Camp* is not an ideological film, but from the opening frames the message is clear: if you value the First Amendment's disestablishment clause, be afraid; if you support a woman's right to terminate a pregnancy through a safe, legal abortion, be terrified.

The film opens in July 2005 with sound bites of talk radio as the camera rolls through Kansas. Supreme Court Justice Sandra Day O'Connor has just announced her retirement, and the sound track cuts from right-wing pundits gleefully speculating on whom the Bush administration will appoint to Evangelical preachers calling on their followers to pray for the appointment of a pro-life associate justice.

Then comes the "not all Christians are like this" scene. The film cuts to the radio studios of Air America's *Ring of Fire*, whose host lawyer, Mike Papantonio, takes calls from listeners upset by the Religious Right, all the while assuring his audience that he "grew up a Christian."

"Something has changed since Matthew wrote, 'Blessed are the peacemakers,'" Papantonio laments, asking what lessons our children derive from contemporary war-like spirituality. However well meaning, the image of a lonely man talking into a microphone does little to change the perception that *Jesus Camp* paints Christianity with large strokes.

The camera's journey through the heartland ends at Christ Triumphant Church in Lee's Summit, Missouri, where a children's revival is taking place. Kids in camouflage face paint are doing an interpretive dance. Each child has a pair of sticks that alternate between being crossed in the form of the most ubiquitous of Christian symbols and being thrust as swords. For the most part, the dance involves marching as the soldiers these kids hope to be.

To Pastor Becky Fischer, the director of Kids in Ministry and the keynote speaker at the Children's Prayer Summit, this is a blessing. The camera shows her pacing the floor in front of a congregation of children and their parents. "Who believes God can do anything?" she asks. The kids stare at her blankly; a few parents lift their children's hands into the air.

"This is a sick old world, and you have to change it!" Now Pastor Becky has the kids' attention. "Do you know that Muslims train their children from the time they're five years old to fast during the month of Ramadan? Listen—we have the keys. We can change the world. Boys and girls can change the world? Absolutely. Hallelujah!" Then everyone (or so it seems) starts speaking in tongues. Kids are crying and shaking on the floor, slain in the Spirit. For Pastor Becky this is normal, to be expected, because kids are more open than adults to the things of God.

The film follows Pastor Becky to Devil's Lake, North Dakota, where her ministry hosts a camp for kids. It's a lot like the children's revival: speaking in tongues, talk about spiritual warfare, warnings against Harry Potter (in the Bible, he would be put to death, Pastor Becky warns the kids), and speakers asking children to give up their lives for the things of Jesus.

Jesus Camp portrays American Christianity with a palpable goofiness. At one point, after the kids have returned from camp, one of the adult leaders brings out a cardboard cutout of George W. Bush and asks the children to pray for the president. They do pray, laying hands on the cardboard image, many of them speaking in tongues, some of them asking God and the president to appoint pro-life judges. That's when abortion starts to take center stage.

After the cardboard cutout of George W. Bush is put away, the Evangelical organizer and pro-life activist Lou Engle (who isn't identified on screen or anywhere in the credits) starts to preach on abortion. And he brings props—little plastic fetus dolls that he passes out to the kids, who join him in prayer, saying, "Jesus, I plead your blood over my sins and the sins of my nation. God, end abortion and bring revival to America!" Everyone starts chanting, "Righteous judges! Righteous judges!"

There are more tongues, more tears, more approving looks from the grown-ups. Then Lou Engle gets out red packing tape and uses it to tape the kids' mouths shut. He writes the word "life" over each pair of sealed lips, an act meant to demonstrate the inability of aborted fetuses to scream. (At this point my wife, who was watching the movie with me, started cussing like a sailor. She stormed off into the kitchen. "For F—'s sake! These kids are six years old!" Thus speaketh the Pastor's Wife.)

Toward the end of the film, *Jesus Camp* goes on the road, first to Ted Haggard's church in Colorado Springs, Colorado (back in the halcyon days before a scandal involving a male prostitute from Denver disgraced the megachurch pastor and erstwhile president of the National Association of Evangelicals), and then to the steps of the Supreme Court building in Washington, D.C. After everyone sings "Nothing but the Blood of Jesus," Engle gives a pep talk, rocking back and forth as he speaks:

> OK. The Bible says that out of the mouths of babes God has ordained praise to silence the enemy and the foe and the avenger. God wants to use the smallest to confound the wise, the things that are nothing to nullify the things that are. You see the big powers here and the big buildings and the big men? God says the prayers of little children can shake *kings*! Come on! Hallelujah!

Then they pray together. The tape is back on their mouths, as silently this group of elementary-school-aged prophets wages spiritual warfare against the powers and principalities of secular liberalism.

Before the movie ends, we return to Air America and the radio studio of *Ring of Fire*. Mike Papantonio is interviewing Pastor Becky. They debate the morality of indoctrinating young children and the merits of democracy. After the interview, Mr. Papantonio takes off his earphones and says with exasperation: "The more I hear about this, . . . it just gets crazier and crazier!"

WHY TALK ABOUT *JESUS CAMP*?

Here I must confess that I loved *Jesus Camp*. It is as good an example of documentary filmmaking as I have seen in a long time; it uses beautiful cinematography, editing, and writing to communicate a message that needs to be heard. But I am bothered by the knowledge that many Americans who are unfamiliar with the broad diversity of American Protestantism will watch *Jesus Camp* and assume that every American Protestant is a pro-life radical who brainwashes kids into becoming zombie soldiers for Christ. It is even worse to think that *Jesus Camp* could be used in countries such as Burma, where Christians are a persecuted minority, as a propaganda tool to build public support for the mistreatment of Christians.

In other words, it would be awful if *Jesus Camp* were to be used against Christians as *Obsession* is used against Muslims.

In the Sermon on the Mount, Jesus admonishes his followers, saying, "in everything do to others as you would have them do to you; for this is the law and the prophets" (Matthew 7:12). This is a Christian articulation of a rule of faith shared by most religious traditions: treat others in the way you want to be treated. It's hard to imagine a Christian wanting a Muslim viewer of *Jesus Camp* to come away from the film thinking that all Christians are pro-life activists who manipulate children. We would want a Muslim viewer of *Jesus Camp* to make the acquaintance of Christians with a firmer grasp of reality and a deeper commitment to rational thought before forming a final opinion of who Christians are.

If, as we relate to our Muslim neighbors, Christians are to apply this golden rule, then we must not assume that *Obesssion*'s claims are the last word on Islam. By equating Islam with one of America's great historical enemies, the makers of *Obsession* invite the movie's viewers to adopt the dangerous propositions that Islam is a religion of violence and Muslims are greatly to be feared. This way of thinking ultimately places Islam on a collision course with other religious traditions and vilifies Muslims who've done nothing more than follow a spiritual path that seems to them to be good and reasonable, a path that in most cases came to them as a legacy of tradition.

If a positive message can be gleaned from *Obsession*, it is this: the heart of Islam cannot be exposed and the world's 1.5 billion Muslims cannot be defined in a mere sixty minutes of biased filmmaking. Those who doubt this message should watch *Jesus Camp* and inquire if that far superior bit of filmmaking has captured the beautiful diversity of the world's Christian community.

Chapter 10

STEALTH JIHAD

And We have sent you universally to all people, as a herald and a warner.

Qur'an 34:28

Go therefore and make disciples of all nations, baptizing them in the name of the Father and of the Son and of the Holy Spirit, and teaching them to obey everything that I have commanded you. And remember, I am with you always, to the end of the age.

Jesus, in Matthew 28:19–20

THE CONVENTION CENTER IN SANTA CLARA, CALIFORNIA, SITS IN the heart of Silicon Valley, and on most nights it plays host to crowds of techies who come from around the world to meet one another at the center of the high-tech universe. They speak the international language of geekdom. They compare iPhone apps in the same way that automotive enthusiasts look under the hoods of cars and appreciate what they see in the greasy half-light that envelops the machinery of internal combustion engines.

But on one night each year, the convention center's largest ballroom becomes a place wholly dedicated to religion, when Muslims from across northern California (many of them among the practitioners of high-tech wizardry that are the Santa Clara Convention Center's regular clientele) gather for the annual fund-raising banquet of Islamic Networks Group (ING). This organization describes itself as "a nonprofit, educational organization . . . that promotes religious literacy and mutual respect through on-site presentations and interfaith dialogues to academic institutions, corporations, health-care facilities, law-enforcement agencies, and other community organizations."[1]

Founded in 1993 "to address the growing misconceptions and misperceptions about Islam and Muslims in the media and among the general public which increased as a result of the political events and issues during and after the First Gulf War,"[2] ING has grown into a nationwide organization with twenty-two affiliates in eighteen states. Each year tens of thousands of people learn about Islam and other religious traditions through the work of ING.

As an expression of ING's commitment to interfaith dialogue, each of its annual fund-raising banquets begins with invocations from each of the three great Abrahamic traditions, and so, in 2009, I attended ING's banquet wearing a clerical collar to pray alongside two colleagues. One wore a yarmulke, and the other—my friend Imam Tahir, to whom I introduced you in chapter 2—came dressed in a traditional *salwar kameez* under a gabardine overcoat.

When it was time for us to pray, Tahir recited a passage from the Qur'an, the rabbi spoke of the importance of tolerance, and I, giving thanks for the millions of religious people around the world who speak kindly of different faith traditions, asked God's blessings upon the gathered crowd.

After the prayers, as we ate dinner, a number of people spoke. Generous donors and interfaith leaders received awards. There was a keynote address by the prominent Islam scholar John Esposito; and Aron Kader, a comedian with a Mormon mother and a Palestinian father, kept us laughing late into the night.

If one theme can be said to have united the speakers that night, it was this: "We want our children to be Americans and to participate fully in the life of their country without feeling ashamed of their religious upbringing."

It seems fair enough. It's hard to imagine anyone in the modern world begrudging American parents for raising their children to be patriotic citizens and leaders in their communities. Yet the work of ING has come under attack[3] because for a growing number of critics of Islam, attempts to make Islam appear to be American, and Muslims to seem mainstream, are considered suspect—evidence that Muslims are trying to subvert the American way of life by acting like "normal" Americans.

STEALTH JIHAD

The sort of people who show up at ING's annual fundraising banquet pose a problem for those who insist that Islam is a faith of violent imperialism. The speakers were eloquent, entirely lacking in the kind of violent vitriol that looks alarming on twenty-four-hour cable news. Absent was any rhetoric condemning America; instead, those who spoke expressed a desire to practice their faith in ways that enhance the vibrant civic life that makes America strong.

The evidence suggests that those who support the work of ING are representative of Islam in America. In 2007, the Pew Research Center, in conducting the "first-ever, nationwide, random sample survey of Muslim Americans, [found] them to be largely assimilated, happy with their lives, and moderate with respect to many of the issues that have divided Muslims and Westerners around the world." American Muslims "are a highly diverse population, one largely composed of immigrants." (American Muslims are 65 percent foreign born; of those born in the United States, 20 percent are African American, and 21 percent are converts to Islam.) Although a majority of American Muslims were not born here, the study found that "they are decidedly American in their outlook, values, and attitudes." They tend to be politically liberal and socially conservative. Just 15 percent of Muslims surveyed for the report had a positive opinion of the then-president George W. Bush, while 61 percent thought that homosexuality should be discouraged.[4] A follow-up study in 2011 found continued political liberalism among American Muslims (70 percent self-identify as Democrats), and a softening on social issues, with only 45 percent of Muslims expressing the opinion that homosexuality should be discouraged.[5]

In response to the clear normalcy of American Muslims, many of Islam's strongest critics have argued that the assimilation of American Muslims is evidence that jihad has gone underground, that Muslims—knowing that they cannot win a war of military force—are subverting the American way of life by living in America as Americans. This is the concept of "stealth" or "soft" jihad: the idea that American Muslims are seeking to create an Islamic state in North America by taking advantage of American laws that require religious accommodation and by manipulating the goodwill of Americans who value religious and cultural diversity so that Islam will be respected and Muslims accepted as mainstream, "regular" Americans.

AN INSIDER'S VIEW

It happens that I know someone who has been accused of engaging in stealth jihad. As the founder and executive director of Islamic Networks Group, Maha ElGenaidi is the person who organizes the annual fund-raising banquets and who invited me to deliver an invocation at the gathering. Maha and I have worked together on a variety of interfaith initiatives, and when I asked if I could talk to her about stealth jihad, she agreed to meet me at her office late on a February afternoon.

The offices of ING are perched near the top of what, in San José, California, counts as a skyscraper. When I arrived after a long elevator ride, Maha greeted me. She was dressed in pink, her cotton blouse matching her hijab (a traditional covering for the hair and neck), which was fashioned from what looked like a Burberry silk scarf. An oversized yet understated and elegant watch kept time on her wrist. She led me into a conference room with a breathtaking view of the Santa Clara Valley, where I began my interview by showing Maha a couple of articles about her work that I had printed out and brought with me. Both articles suggested that Maha's work through ING is a clear example of stealth jihad.[6] I asked her what she made of such accusations. She laughed, picked up the printed pages, looked them over, and thought for a while before telling me that people like her— educated and articulate Muslims who are both theologically orthodox and active in their communities and in America's civic life—pose the greatest threat to those who don't want

Muslims or Islam to have any influence or role to play in American society. "People like me pose a threat because we are normal," she told me, twisting the watch on her wrist.

"I'm out there building relationships with people in community, in corporations, in schools and universities, in law enforcement. That means that I'm mainstreaming Muslims in this country, and there are people who are threatened by that because I am normalizing Islam. That threatens these people, so they vilify me and raise doubts about me in people's minds."

Doubts can be raised even in the minds of those who have no reason to doubt. Maha told me about some of her relatives in Egypt who Googled her and discovered the same articles I'd brought with me. They were afraid Maha was, indeed, engaged in something subversive. "My relatives were horrified by what they read in these articles," she told me. "I had to explain to them what was going on here in America and why these articles are written the way that they are."

The doubts raised by the articles I brought in were particularly troubling to Maha because her Egyptian relatives aren't the only ones Googling her. "Let's say you're using Google, looking for a speaker on Islam, and you see these articles, you're not likely to use us," she explained. Which may be exactly what was intended.

"So," I asked her, "if you're not engaged in stealth jihad, what are you doing?"

Maha told me that her work with ING is motivated by a desire to help Americans understand what Islam really is about. "The American people have a right to know the truth," she told me. "When Americans of another faith get to know who I am, they usually think that I'm an exception, and I'm not. The majority of Muslims are like this—around the world, not just in America."

Maha adjusted her hijab just a bit and told me that her motivation for interfaith work comes from a desire to increase Islamic literacy, and the best way to increase Islamic literacy is to raise awareness about all religious traditions. "I realize that other faith communities are suffering from the same thing that Muslims are suffering from," she told me. "There is a deep misunderstanding in the general public toward them, particularly the Buddhists and the Hindus; and Jews have always suffered from anti-Semitism and still do in this country. I think it's better to go out into the community with people of other faiths rather than just having Muslims go out alone because perceptions of Islam aren't getting any better; in fact, they're getting worse."

Noting the fact that Maha's photo is displayed prominently in one of the articles, I asked her if she had ever received threats from folks who suggest that she is engaged in stealth jihad. She acknowledged the possibility of danger in her work but was determined to continue. Maha looked down at the fine grain of the wooden tabletop that separated us.

"I feel badly for the innocent people who are receiving [the stealth jihad garbage] and who believe it. That has always been my interest. I think the American people, being the absolutely decent people that we are, deserve better. American people, deep down, are good people: they're decent, hardworking people, and they deserve better, and that's why I do the work I do."

The setting winter sun cast a gentle, yellow glow on the hills east of San José as Maha and I finished our interview. On the elevator ride down from the offices of ING, I said a prayer of thanksgiving for the work of people like Maha, Muslims who help Christians like me shed our ignorance and fear.

THE THIRD JIHAD

There is, after all, no shortage of ignorance and fear in the ways that Americans—Christians included—misunderstand Islam.

In 2009, following the wide distribution and media attention generated by the film *Obsession*, its creators released a second movie called *The Third Jihad: Radical Islam's Vision for America*. This documentary's central tenet seems to be that Muslims cannot be trusted even—and perhaps especially—when they are acting in ways that appear entirely trustworthy.

The Third Jihad is a menacing film that pushes viewers' emotional buttons. At first it seems to be a rearticulation of *Obsession*. It puts a good bit of time into making sure that the viewer is aware of the dangers of extremist Muslims who want to take over the world, but then introduces a new twist. The narrator, it turns out, is a Muslim from Arizona—a physician named Zuhdi Jasser. He claims that radical Islam's strategies for taking over the world are not just violent. Rather, radical Islam is attempting to subvert the American way of life simply by *participating* in the American way of life.

"In today's context there are two different kinds of jihad," Dr. Jasser informs us, as what appear to be PowerPoint graphics swirl across the screen. "There is the violent jihad, where the Islamists use violence and terror to try to overthrow their enemies, and then there's been what's termed the 'cultural jihad,' where these Islamists use, in a most duplicitous way, the laws and the rights they have been given in our society to try to work against society and to overthrow it."

By way of putting a face on this threat, the film takes the viewer to New York City, to the periphery of the Muslim Day Parade. There we meet a young man named Yousef Khattab, a supporter of the Islamic Thinkers Society, who appears on camera wearing a slightly rounder version of Malcolm X's glasses, a white skull cap, and a very Amish-looking beard. "Islam will dominate," Khattab proclaims:

> We want to see sharia here, and it will be. The flag of "[there is no other God but Allah, Muhammad is the messenger of God]" will be, inshallah [God willing], on the White House if that's where we choose it to be. It just takes time. The American people are waking up now. . . . There's no compulsion in religion: that means we cannot force it on you, but we will force Islamic sharia law, inshallah.

Abu Mujahid, another member of the Islamic Thinkers Society, takes a more spiritual view: "Allah does say that the whole world will be, eventually, under his ruling. The world will come down to where everyone obeys his laws. It's as simple as that."

The Islamic Thinkers Society is a tiny outfit whose Web site describes the organization as being "less than a handful of Muslims" who evangelize by holding up signs and passing out religious tracts in Times Square,[7] yet size seems not to matter much to the makers of *The Third Jihad*. For the purposes of the film, it is good enough that the members of The Islamic Thinkers Society appear to be endowed with sufficient kookiness to illustrate *The Third Jihad*'s point in an alarming way. They are a fringe group of American Muslims exercising their constitutional right to talk about their religious convictions and political aspirations to anyone in Times Square who is willing to listen. That few people actually are listening to the Islamic Thinkers Society seems immaterial.

To be fair, *The Third Jihad* also warns against the work of larger, more mainstream organizations such as the Council on American-Islamic Relations (CAIR) and the Islamic Society of North America (ISNA), warning against their attempts to make Islam seem like a mainstream, entirely American religion. But whether the movie is talking about a small group of extremists such as the Islamic Thinkers Society or large mainstream Muslim organizations such as CAIR and ISNA, the message is the same: Muslims are scheming to take over America by following American laws and by taking advantage of the rights guaranteed in the U.S. Constitution.

ROBERT SPENCER: GURU OF FEAR

The filmmakers at the Clarion Fund did not invent the idea that Muslim extremists are working legally and nonviolently to establish an Islamic state in North America. Such paranoia has many advocates, but the chief guru of this fear seems to be Robert Spencer, a writer with an impressive résumé that includes ten books, two of which were *New York Times* bestsellers. According to an online bio, Spencer "has led seminars on Islam and jihad for the United States Central Command, United States Army Command and General Staff College, the U.S. Army's Asymmetric Warfare Group, the FBI, the Joint Terrorism Task Force, and the U.S. intelligence community," as well as the U.S. State Department and the German Foreign ministry. He has made dozens of appearances on national and international television and radio broadcast venues and has had speaking engagements at several of America's top colleges and universities.[8]

In addition to his work as a writer, speaker, and media personality, Robert Spencer is the editor of *Jihad Watch*, a Web site subsidiary of *FrontPage Magazine*, published by the David Horowitz Freedom Center. The magazine's editor, David Horowitz, has made a name for himself as a former-leftist-turned-conservative activist who is perhaps most famous for fighting those with pro-Palestinian sentiments on American college and university campuses. *Jihad Watch* speaks of itself as being "dedicated to bringing public attention to the role that jihad theology and ideology play in the modern world and to correcting popular misconceptions about the role of jihad and religion in modern-day conflicts."[9]

In January 2010, *Jihad Watch's* Web site contained a video clip showing Muslim relief workers setting up tents for people displaced by the earthquake in Haiti;[10] this, apparently, is cause for alarm. Another article raised concerns over the fact that a publicly funded educational organization in New Hampshire had been teaching Muslim children from Somalia about the Qur'an. Despite the fact that the program had been put on hold pending an investigation (evidence that the First Amendment still has teeth in the gears of its machinery), for Spencer the idea that Somali children were reading the Qur'an in the Granite State is evidence of Islam's creep into the mainstream. "Welcome to the new New Hampshire!" he writes, as if religious indoctrination of children never occurred in New Hampshire before followers of Islam moved into New England.[11]

If Robert Spencer is the chief guru of fear around stealth jihad, then the "sutra" of this fear—the text of highest authority on the topic—is Spencer's book *Stealth Jihad: How Radical Islam Is Subverting America without Guns or Bombs*. In *Stealth Jihad* Spencer warns of Islam's quiet encroachment on the American way of life. According to Spencer,

> The bottom line is this: there is a concerted effort in America today by Islamic organizations to further a series of initiatives that are outwardly quite different in their stated purposes, and are being advanced by different groups of people. However, they are all geared toward the same set of goals: to encourage Americans to downplay anti-terror initiatives, accommodate Muslim practices, and make special exceptions for Islamic law—while being cowed by cries of "bigotry" into dropping all resistance to these phenomena.
>
> The result, if things continue in this vein, would be an America completely subjugated under Islamic law, . . . an America in which non-Muslims must humble themselves before Muslims, not daring to say or do anything that they find offensive.
>
> This stealth jihad is advancing steadily and quietly, and most Americans have no idea it is happening at all.[12]

Muslims are not the only people of faith to seek accommodation in American life. In my children's school in San José, celebrations of Halloween and even of birthdays must be downplayed out of deference to the sensibilities of a minority of students who are Jehovah's Witnesses. In 2006, Hindu activists in California unsuccessfully challenged the content of sixth-grade social studies textbooks that portrayed India's caste system in a negative light.[13] In December 2009, at the request of a local Hasidic community, bicycle lanes were removed from the Williamsburg neighborhood in Brooklyn so that female cyclists in spandex could not offend the religious sensibilities of the neighborhood's residents.[14]

These examples of religious accommodation—both successful and attempted—are not covered in Spencer's book, but it's safe to assume that he would not see such nods to religious pluralism as a Zionist conspiracy, an expression of Hindu supremacy, or a crafty scheme to get the students in my children's school to purchase *The Watchtower*. For Spencer, Islam is different.

THE PLAN

Both the makers of *The Third Jihad* and Robert Spencer base their fears of a stealth jihad upon the "discovery" of a secret document allegedly produced by the American branch of a worldwide Muslim organization called the Muslim Brotherhood. The Muslim Brotherhood began in Egypt in 1928 and, according to Georgetown scholar John L. Esposito, its founders

> proposed Islam as the organizational and religious solution to poverty and assistance to the dispossessed and downtrodden. Its founder, Hasan al-Banna, taught a message of social and economic justice, preaching particularly to the poor and uneducated. In al-Banna's vision, Islam was not just a philosophy, religion or cultural trend but a social movement seeking to improve all areas of life, not only those that were inherently religious. That is, rather than being simply a belief system, Islam was a call to social action.[15]

Spencer describes the work of the Muslim Brotherhood quite differently. According to Spencer, the Muslim Brotherhood, though it gave birth to the terrorist groups Hamas and al Qaeda, is not just a group that advocates blood, death, and terror. Rather, the Brotherhood has a double identity through which it has become an instrument of stealth jihad. "It takes the form of groups that appear outwardly to be moderate, but advance the *jihadist* agenda through various non-violent initiatives—even while the groups themselves and many of those involved in them have ties to violent *jihadist* organizations."[16]

Either way, in 1991, American members of the Muslim Brotherhood apparently wrote and distributed a fifteen-page paper called "An Explanatory Memorandum on the General Strategic Goal for the Group in North America Outlining a Strategy for Building a Strong and Influential Islamic Community in North America."[17] The paper claims to set down a plan to implement the Brotherhood's goal of the

> enablement of Islam in North America, meaning: establishing an effective and a stable Islamic Movement led by the Muslim Brotherhood which adopts Muslims' causes domestically and globally, and which works to expand the observant Muslim base, aims at unifying and directing Muslims' efforts, presents Islam as a civilization alternative, and supports the global Islamic State wherever it is.[18]

That this document has caused such alarm among American detractors of Islam is puzzling. As far as I know, it is only available online as a PDF document, written in Arabic, with an English translation. The author is not identified, nor is any real publication information given. In other words, the paper cannot be authenticated by a casual reader, but I suspect it is genuine because it is banal. If someone wanted to create a forgery to scare Americans—some sort of "protocol of the elders of Islam," they could have done a much better job.

The paper has one alarming sentence: "The [Brotherhood] must understand that their work in America is a kind of grand jihad in eliminating and destroying the Western civilization from within and 'sabotaging' its miserable house by their hands and the hands of the believers so that it is eliminated and God's religion is made victorious over all other religions." These are nasty words, but they also have a familiar ring. Like many American Christians, I grew up in a Protestant church in which military metaphors were used to describe the work of evangelism and the struggle to live faithfully. Like many Protestants, I grew up singing such hymns as

> Stand up, stand up for Jesus, ye soldiers of the cross; Lift high His royal banner, it must not suffer loss. From victory unto victory His army shall He lead, Till every foe is vanquished, and Christ is Lord indeed.[19]

With their clear reference to the Crusades, the words of the hymn "Stand Up, Stand Up for Jesus" would be about as welcome in the Muslim world as the single, shocking sentence from the Muslim Brotherhood's secret document is to Americans. This is a ubiquitous religious problem: too many of us speak of our faith in militaristic terms, and while we're eager to point out that within the context of our own religious traditions, the violent language is metaphor, we often remain unwilling to see as symbolic the violent language employed by adherents of other faith traditions.

Whatever the intent of this lone alarming sentence, the document's scheme rests on the assumption that if Muslims in North America could mobilize themselves and build strong community organizations, vibrant mosques, and excellent schools, Islam would become a dominant force in American life.

The document seems to have been penned by individuals who have seriously underestimated the power of Lady Gaga, monster-truck rallies, Disney princesses, and countless other cultural trivialities to stifle the religious impulse of the American people. If there's a religious movement powerful enough to displace consumerism and passive entertainment as the dominant force in American life, I don't know about it. Christians have been trying for years to accomplish exactly what the Muslim Brotherhood apparently sets out to do in the document that has people so scared. For generations, Christians of every variety have been trying to transform society by building bigger, better churches and educational institutions. We've branched out into a variety of broadcast, print, and online media. We have best-selling authors and top-forty recording artists. We have world-class athletes proclaiming the gospel. Christians have politicians in the highest and most powerful positions in the world, and the net result is that I cannot get some members of my congregation to show up on Sunday if the 49ers are playing during a losing season—and that's in the age of TiVo. Anyone who thinks he or she can subvert the American way of life using a strategy that can be written out in fifteen pages is delusional.

Nonetheless, those who raise concerns about stealth jihad claim that Muslim operatives have made great strides toward the goal of destroying American civilization and establishing Islam as North America's dominant cultural force. Robert Spencer, for example, claims that the subversive Muslims are "working energetically to wear away the very fabric of American culture. It's happening right now under our noses."[20] To defend his claim that Muslims are taking over America on the sly, Spencer devotes much of his book to a description of American Muslims acting like American Christians, as if such behavior is suspicious or un-American.

For example, Spencer sees evidence of stealth jihad when Muslims condemn what they consider to be offensive portrayals of Islam. When, for example, Muslims protest writings by conservatives such as Charles Krauthammer or Steven Emerson, or even Spencer himself (he dedicates a bit of ink to the ways in which Muslims have pushed back against his work), Spencer sees this as suppressing free speech rather than participation in the give-and-take of public debate.[21] When Muslims organize to fight defamation and to provide legal protections for members of the Muslim community, it demonstrates Muslim contempt for American mores and practices, which are seen as being inferior to those brought to America by Muslims.[22] In response to the Muslim demands for accommodation in public schools, universities, and other public spaces, Spencer warns that "segregation is back in American public schools, aided and abetted by multiculturalist ideologues, thanks to the ideology of Islamic supremacism that holds unbelievers to be unworthy of casual contact with Muslims."[23]

The fact that some banks have agreed to lend money in accordance with Islamic law[24] also makes Spencer suspicious. "Instead of assimilating into American society," he protests, "Muslims are demanding and receiving parallel financial institutions that reinforce the idea that they are unique, not subject to the laws and norms to which the rest of us are subject."[25]

And don't get Robert Spencer started on schools. Muslims can't win: When they work within public schools, they are guilty of stealth jihad. When they start private schools, they are guilty of being aloof supremacists, and anytime anything positive is said about Islam in the world of higher education, it is propaganda that stifles free speech.

Robert Spencer and the filmmakers who created *Stealth Jihad* are not the only pundits warning against stealth jihad. For example, when the New York City Department of Education decided to open the Khalil Gibran Academy, a dual-immersion Arabic and English high school in Brooklyn, historian, activist, and syndicated columnist Daniel Pipes warned that "Arabic-language instruction is inevitably laden with pan-Arabist and Islamist baggage."[26] (The fact that the founders of the school chose to name the academy after a Christian poet might have alerted Pipes and other detractors to the possibility that the school was not intended to be used as an instrument of Muslim evangelism—but never mind.) Through the extensive reach of his column and his Web site, Pipes was able to lead a movement that culminated in the resignation of the school's founding principal.[27]

And when cab drivers in Minneapolis refused to give rides to people carrying alcohol, Glenn Beck—now an independent commentator and former Fox News personality, then a commentator on CNN—declared that sharia law was being forced down American throats and that such accommodation created a "two-tiered justice system."[28]

The issue of stealth jihad has been covered by a wide range of conservative commentators and writers including Michelle Malkin, Pat Robertson, Bill O'Reilly, and Sean Hannity.[29] Maha ElGenaidi once told me that the canard of stealth jihad is one of the most common misconceptions about Islam that is addressed by ING.

THE CHRISTIAN JIHAD

One wonders if Robert Spencer or other writers who warn about stealth jihad have ever taken a critical look at Christianity. Perhaps Spencer and his fellow travelers don't remember the uproar that rippled across the Christian landscape in 1988 after the release of Martin Scorsese's film *The Last Temptation of Christ*. Maybe they aren't aware of the Christian protests that have erupted when an American museum shows an exhibition of Robert Mapplethorpe's photography. Perhaps they have never heard American Christians' demand that creationism and/or "intelligent design" be taught in public high schools as a valid alternative to evolution.

In several states, Christians are lobbying to change public education standards so that they reflect conservative Christian perspectives on history and on the origins of life. Those unwilling to wait for a transformation in the way public schools teach such subjects may send their children to private Christian elementary and secondary schools, which exist in nearly every American city and town. Christian colleges, universities, and seminaries are hard to miss (I hold degrees from two such institutions), and if being set apart while receiving an education isn't enough, Christians can watch Christian television twenty-four hours a day and can go to the cinema to watch Christian movies. For those who would rather not vacation with the unsaved, Christian cruises are available,[30] and for those in search of sanctified fun for the whole family, Christians can attend the Christian-oriented Night of Joy at Disney World.[31]

In fact, when it comes to spreading influence and seeking to change society in accordance with religious norms, Christians go far beyond anything American Muslims have ever attempted. It's hard to imagine how non-Muslim Americans might respond if American Muslims acted like American Christians. If a Muslim organization tried to do something similar to what Promise Keepers used to do, for example, by filling up American sports arenas with testosterone-soaked, spiritually charged men singing the Muslim equivalent of "Rise Up, O Men Of God," it would cause widespread panic. If a Muslim version of Young Life sent volunteers into public high schools to evangelize non-Muslim youth, or if a Muslim version of the Gideons were to leave free copies of the Qur'an in every American hotel room, many American Christians would suddenly find a new devotion to the idea that the First Amendment actually does establish a wall of separation between mosque and state.

A DILEMMA RESOLVED BY FRIENDSHIP

The specter of stealth jihad places Muslims between the horns of an impossible dilemma. Muslims who don't assimilate or participate in American culture are considered to be suspect by their neighbors and coworkers. Those who do participate in the fullness of American life are viewed with suspicion, as if a mainstream existence in America is a ruse if it involves participation in the worshiping life of a local mosque, reading the Qur'an, or saying one's prayers while facing Mecca.

The dilemma faced by our Muslim neighbors presents American Christians with an important choice: Will we live fearfully, assuming that every time American society changes to accommodate the needs of our Muslims neighbors, it is a threat to the prominence of Christianity in the American religious landscape, or will we welcome opportunities to embrace Muslims as full participants in the religious and cultural life of our nation? The first choice places us on the broad path that leads to conflict and dissension; the latter option follows the narrow path that leads to peace.

In the early stages of this chapter's development, I had lunch with a friend who is a lay leader in the San Francisco Bay Area's largest mosque. I asked him about stealth jihad and the possibility that he and other Muslims are trying to take over American society through assimilation and participation in American life. He laughed and took a bite of his vegetarian sandwich (a menu option meant to accommodate Hindus, Muslims, Jews, and vegans). "How long have I known you, Ben, and how many times have I tried to convert you to Islam?" he asked.

I took a bite of my ham sandwich and smiled back, enjoying his company. For the record, that afternoon we'd been friends for eight years and he'd tried to convert me exactly as many times as I'd shared the gospel with him.

Which is how it should be for all of us.

CONCLUSION

The Work Continues

I BEGAN THIS PROJECT IN 2010 WITH THE CONVICTION THAT Americans were living in an historical moment of fear, and I wanted to speak a calming word to that fear. The terrorist attacks of 2001 had altered our lives, we were fighting two wars, the economy was in a deep recession, and partisan gridlock had rendered Washington's corridors of power impotent.

In such times of anxious pessimism, we who are human often look for scapegoats, populations upon which to place the burden of our fearfulness, folks we might punish because of our own helplessness. Judging by the laws and constitutional amendments that were enacted in several of our states at the cusp of the twenty-first century's second decade— statutes that prohibited same-sex marriage, criminalized undocumented migration, and barred the use of sharia in our courts—Americans tended to choose gay men and lesbians, immigrants, and Muslims to be our surrogate enemies. The surrogates were to stand in for the foes—some real, some intangible—that we could not bear to face.

While working on this book, I hoped and prayed that the words contained herein would become unnecessary before the writing of them was completed, that we would overcome our irrational fear and work to solve the real issues that affect us; but these dreams have not come true.

In the spring of 2012, during this book's final editing process, a special edition of *Decision* magazine arrived on my desk. *Decision* is a publication of the Billy Graham Evangelistic Association, and as such it bears upon its glossy cover the imprimatur of the most beloved and trusted name in the world of American Evangelical Protestantism. This special issue of *Decision* was dedicated to covering what it called "Radical Islam's Global War on Christians."

The editorial content of that issue of *Decision* was summed up in a letter from Franklin Graham—son of Billy and current leader of his father's ministries—which accompanied the magazine. In the letter Mr. Graham wrote, "As I have traveled the world, preaching and sharing the Gospel, I have seen firsthand the rising global threat of radical Islam in the Middle East, as well as in parts of Africa and Asia. Frighteningly, I believe it has also become a clear and present danger here in the United States, as courts and lawmakers continue to ignore and reject our Judeo-Christian heritage."[1]

On the same spring day that the postal service delivered *Decision* to me, Anders Breivik went on trial in Norway for the murder of seventy-seven people, many of them teenagers. Breivik had carried out this massacre in the name of defending

Europe from Islam. While the timing was a coincidence, and there was nothing overtly violent in *Decision*, I was struck by the convergence of Breivik's return to the pages of the morning paper and Franklin Graham's dissemination of fear. Clearly, the good people at the Billy Graham Evangelistic Association had failed to learn the lesson so tragically made manifest in Breivik's murderous rampage: fear begets violence.

And so in the spring of 2012, as I was applying the final spit and polish to this manuscript, I came to believe this book was still needed. Yet I cannot end without some token of hope. As a person of faith, I find that hope in the wisdom of the Psalms, which invite us to

> Come, behold the works of the LORD;
> see what desolations he has brought on the earth.
> He makes wars cease to the end of the earth;
> he breaks the bow, and shatters the spear;
> he burns the shields with fire.
> "Be still, and know that I am God!
> I am exalted among the nations,
> I am exalted in the earth."
>
> Psalm 46:8–10

For me, it is a matter of religious conviction that humanity is called to set aside fear—to "be still and know" that God is God—and with courageous hope, to work toward a world in which God destroys our weapons and incapacitates our instruments of fear.

The knowledge that I am not alone in my longings for a better, less fearful, more peaceful world comforts me. The God who answers to a great variety of names, the God who is present to us even when unbidden and unrecognized, will, in the fullness of time, lead us into a world where God's peace will be as irresistible as God's grace.

NOTES

Acknowledgments

1. Kari Huus, "'Islamic Radicalization' Hearing Stirs Hornets' Nest," NBCNews.com, March 9, 2011, http://www.msnbc.msn .com/id/41958327/ns/us_news-security/t/islamic-radicalization -hearing-stirs-hornets-nest/#.T-jnUL8cqg0.

Introduction

1. In the writing of this brief biography of my aunt, I have relied on family lore augmented by the book *In Search of Donna Reed*, by Jay Fultz (Iowa City: University of Iowa Press, 1998).
2. It is Muslim-sounding, anyway. Hussein certainly is a common Muslim name; the name Obama is Kenyan, and as for Mr. Obama's first name, the root of the word "Barack" (variously spelled) means "blessing" in Arabic and Hebrew. If Barack/Barak is an exclusively Muslim name, I think that

former Israeli Prime Minister Ehud Barak might be alarmed to discover it.

3. Dan Gilgoff, "At Debate, Republican Candidates Spar over Islam," CNN.com, June 13, 2011, http://religion.blogs.cnn .com/2011/06/13/at-debate-republican-candidates-spar-over -islam/.

4. Ibid.

5. Ibid.

6. Though "reconquest" is commonly used to describe Catholic Spain's eventually successful efforts to unify Spain under the rule of Roman Catholic monarchs, I don't like the term because it reflects a particular historical point of view. Prior to the "reconquest," no part of southern Spain was governed by rulers that were both Spanish and Christian. It's hard to imagine a "reconquest" when there never was an original conquest to be reprised. There is, however, no other commonly used name for the "reconquest." For more on this, see chapter 6.

7. *Daily Mail Reporter*, "'We Could Have Another Timothy McVeigh': U.S. Authorities Warned against Anti-Islamic Terrorism after Norway Shooter 'Inspired' by Robert Spencer and Unabomber," Mail Online, July 27, 2011, http://www.dailymail.co.uk/ news/article-2018976/Norway-shooting-Anders-Behring-Breivik -inspired-Robert-Spencer-Unabomber.html.

8. See http://www.document.no/anders-behring-breivik/.

9. William Saletan, "Christian Terrorism: If Muslims Are Responsible for Islamic Terrorism, Are Muslim-Bashers Responsible for the Massacre in Norway?" Slate, July 25, 2011, http://www .slate.com/articles/news_and_politics/frame_game/2011/07/ christian_terrorism.html.

10. See John 8:32.

Part 1—Basics: What Is Islam?

1. "Qur'an" is an Arabic word with several different transliterations. In English the title of Islam's holy book can be spelled Koran, Quran, or Qur'an. In this book I use Qur'an because that is the spelling used by most English-speaking Muslim scholars.

2. Seyyed Hossein Nasr, *The Heart of Islam: Enduring Values for Humanity* (San Francisco: HarperSanFrancisco, 2002), 61.

Chapter 1: The City of God

1. From verse 1 of the hymn "Glorious Things of Thee Are Spoken," written by John Newton in 1779, *The Presbyterian Hymnal: Hymns, Psalms and Spiritual Songs* (Louisville, KY: Westminster John Knox Press, 1990), #446

2. A good example of such rhetoric can be found in an essay published on Robert Spencer's Web site *Jihad Watch* by Hugh Fitzgerald, "Fitzgerald: Christianity and Islam: More in Common than Differences?" *Jihad Watch,* October 17, 2005, http://www.jihadwatch.org/2005/10/fitzgerald-christianity-and-islam-more-in-common-than-differences.html.

3. Mr. Nuseibeh's British spelling "Sepulchre," a remnant of the days when the Holy Land was part of the "empire upon which the sun never set," is generally used in the name for that church.

4. I interviewed Wajeeh Nuseibeh on July 6, 2010.

5. Zoé Oldenbourg, *The Crusades* (New York: Pantheon Books, 1966), 151–52.

6. That the Israeli government discriminates against Palestinians in the issuance of building permits has been documented by human rights organizations. See B'Tselem: The Israeli Information Center for Human Rights in the Occupied Territories, "East Jerusalem: Discrimination in Planning, Building, and Land Expropriation," *btselem.org,* January 1, 2011, http://www.btselem.org/jerusalem/discriminating_policy; and Human Rights Watch, "Israel: Stop East Jerusalem Home Demolitions," *Human Rights Watch.org,* November 6, 2009, http://www.hrw.org/news/2009/11/06/israel-stop-east-jerusalem-home-demolitions. This has been reported in Israeli and U.S. media; see Akiva Eldar, "Discrimination Is Flourishing in East Jerusalem," *Haaretz,* May 3, 2010, http://www.haaretz.com/print-edition/opinion/discrimination-is-flourishing-in-east-jerusalem-1.287733; and Howard Schneider, "U.N. Finds 60,000 Palestinians Risk Eviction in East Jerusalem," *Washington Post,* May 2, 2009, http://www.washingtonpost.com/wp-dyn/content/article/2009/05/01/AR2009050103683.html.

Chapter 2: A Muslim Patriot Acts

1. Verse 4 of the hymn "America the Beautiful," written by Katherine Lee Bates in 1895, *The Presbyterian Hymnal,* #564.

2. See the company's Web site: www.salikproductions.com.

3. Khadja Ahman et al., for CAIR, *The Status of Muslim Civil Rights in the United States: Seeking Full Inclusion* (Washington, DC: Council on American Islamic Relations, 2009), 8, http://www.cair.com/Portals/0/pdf/CAIR-2009-Civil-Rights-Report.pdf.

4. Steven Greenhouse, "Muslims Report Rising Discrimination at Work," *New York Times*, September 23, 2010, http://www.nytimes.com/2010/09/24/business/24muslim.html?pagewanted=all.

5. The Anti-Defamation League, "Anti-Muslim Bigotry since 9/11: ADL's Efforts to Address Anti-Muslim Bigotry," *ADL.org*, August 26, 2011, http://www.adl.org/main_Extremism/911_anti_muslim_bigotry.htm?Multi_page_sections=sHeading_4.

6. Dena Sher, "Congress: Stop Targeting American Muslims and Protect Muslim Service Members," *American Civil Liberties Union: Blog of Rights*, December 7, 2011, http://www.aclu.org/blog/national-security/congress-stop-targeting-american-muslims-and-protect-muslim-service-members.

7. Southern Poverty Law Center, "Intelligence Files: Anti-Muslim," *splcenter.org*, http://www.splcenter.org/get-informed/intelligence-files/ideology/anti-muslim.

8. The editors, "Increase in Crimes against Muslims," *Amnesty International USA: Human Rights Now Blog*, September 10, 2010, http://blog.amnestyusa.org/us/increase-in-crimes-against-muslims/.

9. Human Rights Watch, "US/New York: Discipline Police Showing Anti-Muslim Film," *hrw.org*, January 26, 2012, http://www.hrw.org/news/2012/01/26/usnew-york-discipline-police-showing-anti-muslim-film.

10. Pew Research Center for the People and the Press, *Muslim Americans: No Signs of Growth in Alienation or Support for Extremism; Mainstream and Moderate Attitudes* (Washington, DC: Pew Research Center, 2011), *People-press.org*, August 30, 2011, http://www.people-press.org/2011/08/30/muslim-americans-no-signs-of-growth-in-alienation-or-support-for-extremism/?src=prc-headline.

11. Eric Black, "Flying Imams in the Rear-View Mirror: What Was the Evidence against Them?" *MinnPost*, October 26, 2009, http://www.minnpost.com/eric-black-ink/2009/10/flying-imams-rear-view-mirror-what-was-evidence-against-them.

12. Jim Barnett, "Delta Air Lines: Two Muslim Religious Lead-

ers Sue Airlines for Discrimination," *CNN.com*, December 19, 2011, http://articles.cnn.com/2011-12-19/travel/travel_us-airlines -imams-suit_1_tsa-agents-plane-religious-leaders?_s=PM:TRAVEL.

13. Ihsan Bagby, for CAIR, *The American Mosque 2011: Basic Characteristics of the American Mosque; Attitudes of Mosque Leaders*, Report Number 1 from the US Mosque Study 2011 (Washington, DC: Council on American-Islamic Relations, January 2012), http://faithcommunitiestoday.org/sites/faithcommunitiestoday .org/files/The%20American%20Mosque%202011%20web.pdf.

Part 2—Basics: Who Is Allah?

1. *The Compact Edition of the Oxford English Dictionary* (New York: Oxford University Press, 1971), 1:57.

2. Marshall G. S. Hodgson, *The Classical Age of Islam*, vol. 1 of *The Venture of Islam: Conscience and History in a World Civilization* (Chicago: University of Chicago Press, 1974), 155–56.

3. Karen Armstrong, *Islam: A Short History* (New York: Modern Library, 2002), 7–8.

Chapter 3: Imam Zaid Shakir and the Education of American Muslims

1. *Dhu al-Hijjah* is the twelfth month in the Islamic year, which follows a lunar calendar.

2. In the Christian and Jewish traditions, the story of Abraham's sacrifice involves his son Isaac. In Islam, the story is basically the same except that Abraham almost sacrifices his son Ishmael.

3. Shafath Syed, from a speech delivered at the *Eid al-Adha* celebrations in San José, California, on November 17, 2010.

4. See http://www.zaytunacollege.org/about/our_name/.

5. Imam Zaid Shakir, "The Making of a Muslim," in *Scattered Pictures: The Reflections of an American Muslim* (Hayward, CA: Zaytuna Institute, 2005), 9–11.

6. I interviewed Imam Zaid Shakir on November 11, 2010.

7. Gentle Reader, if you are lost, take heart: you're not alone. I had to consult *Wikipedia* (http://en.wikipedia.org/wiki/ Dialectical_materialism) to understand dialectical materialism.

People like you and me may derive some consolation in knowing that, in another century, our failing grasp of Marxist historical analysis might have protected us from prosecution by the House Committee on Un-American Activities.

8. Maria Zain, "Islamic Education in the US: Its Growth, Demand and Developments," *DinarStandard.com*, June 30, 2011, http://dinarstandard.com/challenges/islamic-education-in-the -us-its-growth-demand-and-developments/.

9. Julie Stolberg, "Duke Aims to Carve Out Niche in Islam Studies," *The Chronicle*, December 4, 2006, http://www .dukechronicle.com/article/duke-aims-carve-out-niche-islam-studies.

10. Jennifer Carnig, "Islamic Studies Programs Thrive at University, as Interest in Islam Grows," *University of Chicago Chronicle*, July 14, 2005, http://chronicle.uchicago.edu/050714/islamic studies.shtml.

Chapter 4: A Jihad Grows in Berkeley (or Not)

1. Roy Zimmerman, "Peace Is Out," © Watunes 1994, from the album *Folk Heroes*, by Foremen [Musical Group] (Burbank, CA: Reprise Records, 1995), http://www.royzimmerman.com/ lyrics/best_peace.html.

2. David Horowitz, *The Professors: The 101 Most Dangerous Academics in America* (Washington, DC: Regency Publishing, 2007), 47–49.

3. The original e-mail that alerted me to this quote by Hatem Bazian has long since disappeared from my life. I found the same quote again in ibid., 47.

4. Steven Emerson, *American Jihad: The Terrorists Living among Us* (New York: Free Press, 2002), 214–15.

5. Safoora Ahmed, "Why Sufism Is Being Demonised by Wahabism," *A Sufi Metamorphosis Blog*, July 13, 2011, http:// zoya-thewayofasufi.blogspot.com/2011/07/why-sufism-is-being-demonised-by.html.

6. Ibid.

7. My information on the Free Speech Movement is compiled from two sources: the online "Free Speech Movement Chronology," first published in *The California Monthly*, February 1965; republished at http://bancroft.berkeley.edu/FSM/chron

.html (© Regents of the University of California); and Seth Rosenfeld, "Mario Savio's FBI Odyssey: How the Man Who Challenged 'The Machine' Got Caught in the Gears and Wheels of J. Edgar Hoover's Bureau," *SFGate.com*, October 10, 2004, 1, http://articles.sfgate.com/2004-10-10/living/17446882_1_mario-savio -hoover-s-fbi-free-speech-movement.

8. Quote from "Free Speech Movement Chronology."

9. Daniel Pipes, "What Is Jihad?" *New York Post*, December 31, 2002; as found on *DanielPipes.org: Middle East Forum*, http:// www.danielpipes.org/990/what-is-jihad.

10. Jim Lobe, "Muslim 'Terror Threat' Belied by Numbers," *Al Jazeera*, February 9, 2012, http://www.aljazeera.com/indepth/ features/2012/02/20122912326479430.html.

11. Raja Abdulrahim, "American Muslim Population Projected to Double by 2030," *Los Angeles Times*, January 28, 2011, http://articles.latimes.com/2011/jan/28/nation/la-na-muslim -report-20110128.

12. John L. Esposito, *What Everyone Needs to Know about Islam* (New York: Oxford University Press, 2002), 182.

13. Imam Zaid Shakir, "Jihad Is Not Perpetual Warfare," *Scattered Pictures: Reflections of an American Muslim* (Hayward, CA: Zaytuna Institute, 2005), 125–26.

14. Seyyed Hossein Nasr, *The Heart of Islam: Enduring Values for Humanity* (San Francisco: HarperSanFrancisco, 2002), 258–59.

15. Ibid., 260.

16. For a comprehensive and detailed report on the purveyors of Islamophobia and those who fund their work, see Wajahat Ali et al., *Fear, Inc.: The Roots of the Islamophobia Network in America* (Washington, DC: Center for American Progress, 2011), eBook, http://www.americanprogress.org/issues/2011/ 08/islamophobia.html. For an advocacy-journalistic perspective, see Max Blumenthal, "The Great Islamophobic Crusade," *MaxBlumenthal.com*, December 20, 2010, http://maxblumenthal.com/ 2010/12/the-great-islamophobic-crusade/. For a peer-reviewed scholarly article on the subject, see Lawrence Davidson, "Islamophobia, the Israel Lobby, and American Paranoia: Letter from America," *Holy Land Studies* 10 (2011): 87–95, http://www .euppublishing.com/doi/abs/10.3366/hls.2011.0005.

17. Anti Defamation League, "Backgrounder: Stop Islamization of America (SIOA)," *adl.org*, March 25, 2011, http://www.adl.org/main_Extremism/sioa.htm.

18. Ali, *Fear, Inc.*, 85–117.

19. Rosenfeld, "Mario Savio's FBI Odyssey," 9.

Part 3—Basics: Who Was Muhammad?

1. John L. Esposito, *What Everyone Needs to Know about Islam* (New York: Oxford University Press, 2002), 12–13, 109–10.

2. Ibid., 116.

Chapter 5: From Muhammad of Mecca to Ray in San José

1. Bob Marley and Noel G. Williams, "Buffalo Soldier," from the album *Confrontation*, Tuff Gong/Island 1983, compact disc.

2. Marshall G. S. Hodgson, *The Classical Age*, vol. 1 of *The Venture of Islam: Conscience and History in a World Civilization* (Chicago: University of Chicago Press, 1974), 152.

3. Fred M. Donner, *Muhammad and the Believers: At the Origins of Islam* (Cambridge, MA: Belknap Press of Harvard University Press, 2010), 33.

4. Ibid., 28–32.

5. Ibid., 34–38.

6. Ibid., 29–31.

7. Ingrid Mattson, *The Story of the Qur'an: Its History and Place in Muslim Life* (Malden, MA: Blackwell Publishing, 2008), 16.

8. Ibid., 18.

9. Qur'an 96:1–5, in *The Qur'an: A New Translation*, trans. by Thomas Clearly (Bridgeview, IL: Starlatch Press, 2004), 298–99.

10. Karen Armstrong, *Islam: A Short History* (New York: Modern Library, 2002), 4.

11. Mattson, *Story of the Qur'an*, 19.

12. Armstrong, *Islam*, 4.

13. Qur'an 2:135–36.

14. Armstrong, *Islam*, 1.

15. John L. Esposito, *What Everyone Needs to Know about Islam* (New York: Oxford University Press, 2002), 23.

16. Mattson, *Story of the Qur'an*, 4.

17. Armstrong, *Islam*,11.
18. Qur'an 29:17a.
19. Donner, *Muhammad and the Believers*, 42.
20. Ibid., 43.
21. See, e.g., Ali Sina, "Aisha: The Child Bride of Muhammad," *AliSina.org Blog*, December 4, 2010, http://alisina.org/blog/2010/12/04/aisha-the-child-bride-of-muhammad.
22. John McLaughlin, "Medieval Child Marriage: Abuse of Wardship?" a paper delivered at Plymouth State College, Plymouth, New Hampshire, Conference on Medieval Studies, April 1997, http://www.thedigitalfolklife.org/childmarriage.htm.
23. See William Shakespeare, *Richard II*, act II, scene 2.
24. Charles Dickens, *A Child's History of England* (New York: Books, Inc., 1936), 153.
25. Armstrong, *Islam*, 15–16.
26. Qur'an 3:103.
27. Armstrong, *Islam*, 14.
28. Ibid., 15.
29. Ibid., 14.
30. Qur'an 29:46.
31. Armstrong, *Islam,* 17.
32. Esposito, *What Everyone Needs to Know*, 81.
33. Armstrong, *Islam*, 18.
34. Hodgson, *Classical Age*, 193–95.
35. Qur'an 8:65.
36. Qur'an 2:190–94.
37. Hodgson, *Classical Age*, 195.
38. Donner, *Muhammad and the Believers*, 50.
39. Hodgson, *Classical Age*, 197.
40. Donner, *Muhammad and the Believers*, 98.
41. Hodgson, *Classical Age*, 200.
42. Ibid., 200.
43. Donner, *Muhammad and the Believers*, 119–25.
44. Armstrong, *Islam*, 31.
45. Donner, *Muhammad and the Believers*, 133.
46. Armstrong, *Islam*, 32.
47. Ibid., 33.
48. Ibid., 33–34.
49. Ibid., 35–36.

50. I am grateful to my friend Samir Laymoun for his help with the translation of the Arabic word *fitna*.

51. Armstrong, *Islam*, 51.

52. Ibid., 43.

53. Esposito, *What Everyone Needs to Know*, 45.

54. "Bahrain News—the Protests," *The New York Times*, June 24, 2012, http://topics.nytimes.com/top/news/international/countries andterritories/bahrain/index.html, updated August 23, 2012.

55. Armstrong, *Islam*, 141–46.

56. William Harold Ingrams, *The Yemen: Imams, Rulers, and Revolutions* (New York: Frederick A. Praeger, 1963), 3–4.

57. Ibid., 37.

58. Robert D. Burrowes, *Historical Dictionary of Yemen*, 2nd ed. (Lanham, MD: Scarecrow Press, 2010), 274–75.

59. Victoria Clark, *Yemen: Dancing on the Heads of Snakes* (New Haven: Yale University Press, 2010), 21.

60. Ibid., 29.

61. "Background Note: Yemen," U.S. Department of State, March 12, 2012, http://www.state.gov/outofdate/bgn/yemen/196398.htm.

62. Clark, *Yemen*, 88.

63. Ibid., 129–30.

64. "Background Note: Yemen," March 12, 2012.

Chapter 6: Córdoba and the Misappropriation of Memory

1. *Lawrence of Arabia*, directed by David Lean (Columbia Pictures, 1962).

2. The editors, "CNN Poll: Most Oppose Mosque near Ground Zero," *CNN Belief Blog*, August 11, 2010, http://religion.blogs.cnn.com/2010/08/11/cnn-poll-most-oppose-mosque-near-ground-zero/.

3. Russell Goldman and Jake Tapper, "Islamic Center 'Ground Zero Mosque' Controversy Heats Up," *ABC News*, August 19, 2010, http://abcnews.go.com/Politics/islamic-center-ground-mosque-controversy-heats/story?id=11435030.

4. Justin Elliott, "How the 'Ground Zero Mosque' Fear Mongering Began," *Salon.com*, Monday, August 16, 2010, http://www.salon.com/news/politics/war_room/2010/08/16/ground_zero_mosque_origins.

5. According to Justin Elliott (ibid.), Pamela Gellar also has written a piece suggesting that Barack Obama is Malcolm X's son. To be entirely accurate, Gellar didn't pen the piece on the president's patrimony, but she did publish it at http://atlasshrugs 2000.typepad.com/atlas_shrugs/2008/10/how-could-stanl.html, so "third-tier" seems entirely appropriate.

6. Pamela Geller, "Giving Thanks," *Atlas Shrugs*, December 8, 2009, http://atlasshrugs2000.typepad.com/atlas_shrugs/2009/12/giving-thanks.html.

7. Anne Barnard and Alan Feuer, "Outraged, and Outrageous," *New York Times*, October 8, 2010, http://www.nytimes.com/2010/10/10/nyregion/10geller.html.

8. Newt Gingrich, "Newt Gingrich Statement on Proposed Mosque/Islamic Community Center near Ground Zero," *Newt.org*, July 21, 2010.

9. From a tourist pamphlet titled *The Cathedral of Córdoba: A Live Witness to Our History* (Córdoba: The Cathedral, n.d.).

10. J. Agustín Núñez, *Córdoba in Focus*, trans. Jon Trout (Granada, Spain: Edilux, 2001).

11. Chris Lowney, *A Vanished World: Muslims, Christians, and Jews in Medieval Spain* (New York: Oxford University Press, 2006), 21–22.

12. Williston Walker et al., *A History of the Christian Church*, 4th ed. (New York: Scribner's Sons, 1985), 131–33.

13. Lowney, *A Vanished World*, 24.

14. María Rosa Menocal, *Ornament of the World: How Muslims, Jews, and Christians Created a Culture of Tolerance in Medieval Spain*, pbk. ed. (New York: Back Bay Books, 2003), 25.

15. Karen Armstrong, *Islam: A Short History* (New York: Modern Library, 2002), 8–10.

16. Menocal, *Ornament of the World*, 7–8.

17. Ibid., 27.

18. Lowney, *A Vanished World*, 66–67.

19. Ibid., 71–74.

20. Menocal, *Ornament of the World*, 34.

21. I'm using quotation marks here because it often is said that the expansion of Catholic Spain into al-Andalus was a reconquest of territory formerly held by Spanish Catholics, yet local Spaniards—as noted earlier in this chapter—had not held political power in the territory since the Roman conquest of the Iberian

Peninsula in 206 BCE, and no one practicing traditional Catholic Christianity had ever ruled Southern Spain, save for a few decades at the tail end of the Visigoth era.

22. Núñez, *Córdoba in Focus*, 10.
23. Menocal, *Ornament of the World*, 72–73.
24. Armstrong, *Islam*, 30–31.
25. Menocal, *Ornament of the World*, 84–87.
26. For a concise, detailed description of anti-Semitism in medieval Europe, see Jonathan Kirsch, *The Grand Inquisitor's Manual: A History of Terror in the Name of God* (San Francisco: HarperOne, 2008), 167–73.
27. Armstrong, *Islam*, 21–22.
28. Lowney, *A Vanished World*, 95.
29. Ibid., 29.
30. Ibid., 145–46.
31. Núñez, *Córdoba in Focus*, 8.
32. Menocal, *Ornament of the World*, 198.
33. Lowney, *A Vanished World*, 193.
34. Daniel C. Matt, *The Essential Kabbalah: The Heart of Jewish Mysticism* (San Francisco: HarperSanFrancisco, 1995), 6–7.

Part 4—Basics: What Is the Qur'an?

1. John L. Esposito, *What Everyone Needs to Know about Islam* (New York: Oxford University Press, 2002), 8–9.
2. Seyyed Hossein Nasr, *The Heart of Islam: Enduring Values for Humanity* (San Francisco: HarperSanFrancisco, 2002), 23.

Chapter 7: Islam and Violence

1. Dana Priest, "CIA Holds Terror Suspects in Secret Prisons," *Washington Post*, November 2, 2005, http://www.washingtonpost.com/wp-dyn/content/article/2005/11/01/AR2005110101644.html.
2. American Civil Liberties Union, "Fact Sheet: Extraordinary Rendition," *Blog of Rights*, http://www.aclu.org/national-security/fact-sheet-extraordinary-rendition.
3. Severin Carrell, "The Children of Guantanamo Bay," *The Independent*, May 28, 2006, http://www.independent.co.uk/news/world/americas/the-children-of-guantanamo-bay-480059.html.

4. David Randall and Emily Gosden, "62,006–180,000—The Number Killed in the 'War on Terror,'" *The Independent*, September 9–10, 2006, http://www.informationclearinghouse.info/article14906.htm.

5. Gilbert Burnham, Riyadh Lafta, Shannon Doocy, and Les Roberts, "Mortality after the 2003 Invasion of Iraq: A Cross-sectional Cluster Sample Survey," *TheLancet.com*, October 12, 2006, http://www.thelancet.com/journals/lancet/article/PIIS0140 -6736%2806%2969491-9/fulltext.

6. When I speak of the "myth" of Muslim violence, I use the word "myth" not as it is popularly used, to denote a lie, but as it is defined by Merriam-Webster, a respected dictionary: "a popular belief or tradition that has grown up around something or someone; *especially*: one embodying the ideals and institutions of a society or segment of society." See *Merriam-Webster's Collegiate Dictionary, Eleventh Edition* (Springfield, MA: Merriam-Webster, 2003), 822.

7. Steve Rendall and Isabel MacDonald, "Making Islamophobia Mainstream: How Muslim-Bashers Broadcast Their Bigotry," *FAIR: Fairness and Accuracy in Reporting*, November/December 2008, http://www.fair.org/index.php?page=3648.

8. Saladin Ahmed, "Muslims in My Monitor," *The Escapist*, August 31, 2010, http://www.escapistmagazine.com/articles/view/issues/issue_269/8044-Muslims-in-My-Monitor.

9. Thomas S. Kidd, *American Christians and Islam: Evangelical Culture and Muslims from the Colonial Period to the Age of Terrorism* (Princeton, NJ: Princeton University Press, 2009), 3–5.

10. Ibid., 2–3.

11. Ibid., 1–30.

12. Frank Lambert, *The Barbary Wars: American Independence in the Atlantic World* (New York: Hill & Wang, 2005), 4.

13. Ibid., 4.

14. Ibid., 4–7.

15. The U.S. war against the Barbary States is largely forgotten, except in the first stanza of the Marine Corps Hymn: "From the halls of Montezuma / To the shores of Tripoli."

16. Kidd, *American Christians and Islam*, 11–12.

17. See, e.g., Joel Richardson, *The Islamic Antichrist: The Shocking Truth about the Real Nature of the Beast* (Los Angeles: WND Books, 2009).

18. The Albigensian Crusades are named for the city of Albi, a Cathar stronghold in the south of France.

19. Williston Walker et al., *A History of the Christian Church*, 4th ed. (New York: Scribner's Sons, 1985), 303.

20. William of Tudela and an anonymous successor, *The Song of the Cathar Wars: A History of the Albigensian Crusades*, trans. Janet Shirley, pbk. ed. (Burlington, VT: Ashgate Publishing, 2000), 1.

21. Jonathan Kirsch, *The Grand Inquisitor's Manual: A History of Terror in the Name of God* (San Francisco: HarperOne, 2008), 43–44.

22. Walker, *History of the Christian Church*, 308.

23. Kirsch, *Grand Inquisitor's Manual*, 48.

24. William of Tudela, *Song of the Cathar Wars*, 21.

25. "Immunity," in *The Catholic Encyclopedia*, vol. 7 (New York: Robert Appleton Co., 1910), copied by *NewAdvent.org*, http://www.newadvent.org/cathen/07690a.htm.

26. Zoé Oldenbourg, *The Crusades*, trans. Anne Carter (New York: Pantheon Books, 1966), 140.

27. Karen Armstrong, *Holy War: The Crusades and Their Impact on Today's World* (New York: Anchor Books, 2001), 386–87.

28. Walker, *History of the Christian Church*, 309–10.

29. For an excellent description of the groups targeted by the Inquisition, see chap. 5, "The Inquisitor's Manual," in Kirsch, *Grand Inquisitor's Manual*, 133–66.

30. Ibid., 54–55.

31. Ibid., 205.

32. Angela Bonavoglia, "American Nuns: Guilty as Charged?" *The Nation*, May 21, 2012, http://www.thenation.com/article/167986/american-nuns-guilty-charged.

33. For examples of Luther's anti-Semitic writing, see Martin Luther, *The Jews and Their Lies* (1543), from *Luther's Works*, vol. 47, *The Christian in Society* IV, ed. Jaroslav Pelikan (Philadelphia: Fortress Press, 1971), 268–93, as excerpted in *The Internet Medieval Sourcebook*, http://www.jewishvirtuallibrary.org/jsource/anti-semitism/Luther_on_Jews.html.

34. Walker, *History of the Christian Church*, 437–38.

35. Ibid., 520–21.

36. Thomas H. L. Parker, *John Calvin: A Biography* (Philadelphia: Westminster Press, 1975), 117–19.

37. Ibid., 120.

38. Williston Walker, *John Calvin: The Organiser of Reformed Protestantism (1509–64)* (New York: Schocken Books, 1969), 325–44; and Alister E. McGrath, *A Life of John Calvin: A Study in the Shaping of Western Culture* (Oxford: Basil Blackwell, 1990), 132.

39. McGrath, *A Life of John Calvin*, 119.

40. Ibid., 119–20.

41. Walker, *History of the Christian Church*, 449.

42. Donald B. Kraybill and Carl Desportes Bowman, *On the Backroad to Heaven: Old Order Hutterites, Mennonites, Amish, and Brethren* (Baltimore: Johns Hopkins Press, 2001), 2.

43. From the Web site of the Grand Orange Lodge of Scotland, http://www.orangeorderscotland.com/.

44. Cathy Hayes, "Orange Order Parade's Spark Further Violence in Northern Ireland," *Irish Central*, July 13, 2010, http://www.irishcentral.com/news/Orange-Order-Parades-spark-further-violence-in-Northern-Ireland-98306414.html.

45. Between the writing and publication of this book, the Rangers, due to financial mismanagement, have been demoted to Scotland's third division.

46. "Offensive Behaviour at Football and Threatening Communications (Scotland) Act 2012," The Scottish Government's official Web site, http://www.scotland.gov.uk/Topics/Justice/law/sectarianism-action-1/football-violence/bill.

47. John L. Esposito, *What Everyone Needs to Know about Islam* (New York: Oxford University Press, 2002), 119–22.

48. Reza Shah-Kazemi, "From the Spirituality of Jihad to the Ideology of Jihadism," *Seasons: Semiannual Journal of Zaytuna Institute* 2, no. 2 (Spring–Summer Reflections, 2005): 49; see the article, http://www.truejihad.com/uploads/jihad-ed2.pdf; or an abridged version, http://www.truejihad.com/pages/true-jihad.php.

49. Zsolt Nyiri, "Muslims in Europe: Basis for Greater Understanding Already Exists," *Gallup*, April 30, 2007, http://www.gallup.com/poll/27409/muslims-europe-basis-greater-understanding-already-exists.aspx.

50. The United States Department of State Office for the Coordination of Counterterrorism, "Country Reports on Terrorism, 2009, Chapter 6, Terrorist Organizations," August 5, 2010, http://www.state.gov/j/ct/rls/crt/2009/140900.htm.

51. To see the odds that you might be dealt four of a kind

or a straight flush in a hand of five-card poker, see http://www
.bobsokol.com/Poker.html.

52. Richard Wike and Nilanthi Samaranayake, "Where Terrorism Finds Support in the Muslim World," *Pew Research Center Publications*, May 23, 2006, http://pewresearch.org/pubs/26/where-terrorism-finds-support-in-the-muslim-world.

53. Karen Armstrong, *Islam: A Short History* (New York: Modern Library, 2002), 164–75.

54. Charles Kimball, *When Religion Becomes Evil* (San Francisco: HarperSanFrancisco, 2002).

55. The exceptions to this rule may be members of the Jain faith, who practice strict nonviolence.

Chapter 8: Islam and Women

1. Karen Armstrong, *Islam: A Short History* (New York: Modern Library, 2002), 15.

2. Robert Spencer, "Honor Killing in Texas," *Human Events*, January 8, 2008, http://www.humanevents.com/article.php?id=24329.

3. Pamela Geller, "Muslims Murder Their Women, Blame Critics of Islam," *Atlas Shrugs*, August 20, 2011, http://atlasshrugs2000.typepad.com/atlas_shrugs/2011/08/muslims-murder-blame-critics-of-islam.html.

4. For an image of the August 9, 2010, issue of *Time* magazine, visit http://www.time.com/time/covers/0,16641,20100809,00.html.

5. Khaled Hosseini, *A Thousand Splendid Suns* (New York: Riverhead Books, 2007).

6. Geraldine Brooks, *Nine Parts of Desire: The Hidden World of Islamic Women* (New York: Anchor Books, 1995).

7. Irshad Manji, *The Trouble with Islam Today: A Muslim's Call for Reform in Her Faith* (New York: St. Martin's Griffin, 2005).

8. Ayaan Hirsi Ali, *Infidel* (New York: Free Press, 2007).

9. Ayaan Hirsi Ali, *Nomad: From Islam to America—A Personal Journey through the Clash of Civilizations* (New York: Free Press, 2010).

10. "Impunity for Domestic Violence, 'Honour Killings' Cannot Continue—UN Official," *UN News Centre*, March 4, 2010, http://www.un.org/apps/news/story.asp?NewsID=33971&Cr=violence+against+women&Cr1.

11. "Culture of Discrimination: A Fact Sheet on 'Honor' Killings," *Amnesty International*, 2012, http://www.amnestyusa.org/sites/default/files/pdfs/vaw_fact_sheet.pdf.

12. "India: Prosecute Rampant 'Honor' Killings," *Human Rights Watch*, July 18, 2010, http://www.hrw.org/news/2010/07/16/india-prosecute-rampant-honor-killings.

13. Anna Momigliano, "Honor Killing by Any Other Name," *The Nation*, February 15, 2010, http://www.thenation.com/article/honor-killing-any-other-name.

14. Rana Husseini, "Honor-Related Crimes in Jordan," *Strengthening Understanding of Femicide: Using Research to Galvanize Action and Accountability*, Program for Appropriate Technology in Health (PATH), InterCambios, Medical Research Council of South Africa (MRC), and World Health Organization (WHO), 2009, 85, http://www.path.org/publications/files/GVR_femicide_rpt.pdf.

15. Julia E. Monárrez Fragoso, "An Analysis of Femicide in Ciudad Juárez: 1993–2007," *Strengthening Understanding of Femicide: Using Research to Galvanize Action and Accountability*, Program for Appropriate Technology in Health (PATH), InterCambios, Medical Research Council of South Africa (MRC), and World Health Organization (WHO), 2009, 81, http://www.path.org/publications/files/GVR_femicide_rpt.pdf.

16. Jennifer Casey and Angélica Cházaro, "Getting Away with Murder: Guatemala's Failure to Protect Women and Rodi Alvarado's Quest for Safety," *Center for Gender & Refugee Studies*, University of California, Hastings College of the Law, November 2005, http://cgrs.uchastings.edu/documents/cgrs/cgrs_guatemala_femicides.pdf.

17. Guatemala Human Rights Commission/USA, "For Women's Right to Live," http://www.ghrc-usa.org/Programs/ForWomensRighttoLive.htm.

18. José Sanmartín Esplungues, Isabel Iborra Marmolejo, Yolanda García Esteve, and Pilar Martínez Sánchez, *Violencia contra la mujer en las relaciones de pareja: Estadísticas y Legislación; III Informe Internacional* (Valencia: Centro Reina Sofía, 2010), 71, http://www.fundacionluisvives.org/upload/88/18/informe.pdf.

19. United Nations Office on Drugs and Crime, "Human Trafficking," *UNODC.org*, 2012, http://www.unodc.org/unodc/en/human-trafficking/what-is-human-trafficking.html.

20. Sandeep Chawla et al., *Global Report on Trafficking in Persons: Human Trafficking a Crime That Shames Us All*, Global Initiative to Fight Human Trafficking (Vienna: United Nations Office on Drugs and Crime, 2009), 11.

21. Ibid., 50.

22. "H.R. 7311 (110th): William Wilberforce Trafficking Victims Protection Reauthorization Act of 2008," *Govtrack.us*, http://www.govtrack.us/congress/bills/110/hr7311.

23. U.S. Department of State, "Trafficking in Persons Report 2009," introduced by Secretary Hillary Clinton, June 16, 2009, http://www.state.gov/j/tip/rls/tiprpt/2009/.

24. Robert Spencer, "Breaking News! Muslim Countries Lead in Human Trafficking," *Jihad Watch*, June 18, 2009, http://www.jihadwatch.org/2009/06/breaking-news-muslim-countries-lead-in-human-trafficking.html.

25. Pamela Geller, "Muslim Countries Lead in Trafficking and Slavery," *Atlas Shrugs*, June 10, 2009, http://atlasshrugs2000.typepad.com/atlas_shrugs/2009/06/muslim-countires-leads-in-trafficking-and-slavery.html (note that "countries" is misspelled in the Web address).

26. U.S. Department of State, "Trafficking in Persons Report 2011," http://www.state.gov/j/tip/rls/tiprpt/2011/index.htm.

27. UN Women, compilers of "Facts & Figures on VAW [Violence against Women]" present data compiled in 2011 for 86 countries, *UN Women*, 2011, http://www.unifem.org/gender_issues/violence_against_women/facts_figures.php?page=5.

28. Simon Rogers, "Maternal Mortality: How Many Women Die in Childbirth in Your Country?" *The Guardian Data Blog*, posted April 13, 2010, http://www.guardian.co.uk/news/datablog/2010/apr/12/maternal-mortality-rates-millennium-development-goals.

29. The World Bank, "Gross National Income per Capita 2010, Atlas Method and PPP," http://siteresources.worldbank.org/DATASTATISTICS/Resources/GNIPC.pdf.

30. Nicholas D. Kristof and Sheryl WuDunn, *Half the Sky: Turning Oppression into Opportunity for Women Worldwide*, Kindle ed. (New York: Alfred A. Knopf, 2009), chap. 7, "Why Do Women Die in Childbirth?"

31. See, e.g., Robert Spencer, "Afghanistan: Islamic Supremacists Poison 97 More Girls for the Crime of Going to School,"

Jihad Watch, June 3, 2012, http://www.jihadwatch.org/2012/06/
afghanistan-islamic-supremacists-poison-97-more-girls-for-the
-crime-of-going-to-school.html.

32. "Education Statistics," in "Literacy—Female by Country," *CIA World Factbooks 18 December 2003 to 28 March 2011*, copy
issued by *NationMaster.com*, http://www.nationmaster.com/
graph/edu_lit_fem-education-literacy-female.

33. Kristof and WuDunn, *Half the Sky*, chap. 9, "Is Islam
Misogynistic?"

34. "Switzerland's Long Way to Women's Right to Vote (In
a Direct Democracy Change Takes a Little Longer)," *History of
Switzerland: Female Suffrage*, 2004, http://history-switzerland
.geschichte-schweiz.ch/chronology-womens-right-vote
-switzerland.html.

35. "This is a compilation of all the verses in [the] Qur'an
that have the word 'women' [or 'woman'] in them," trans.
M[ohammedali Habib] Shakir, "all verses taken out of context," apparently from *The Noble Qur'an: A New Rendering of Its
Meaning in English* (New York: Tahirke Tarsile Qur'an, 1999),
jannah.org, 1995–2012, http://www.jannah.org/sisters/177
.html.

36. Qur'an 4:11.

37. Qur'an 2:282.

38. Qur'an 4:3.

39. Qur'an 2:222.

40. Qur'an 24:30.

41. 'Allamah Muhammad Jawad Maghniyyah, "The Rules
of Modesty according to Five Islamic Schools of Law,"
Al-Islam.org, http://www.al-islam.org/encyclopedia/chapter7/
2.html.

42. See "Psalm 127:3–5: 'Lo, Children are an Heritage of
the Lord . . .,'" *QuiverFull Resources*, 1995–2012, http://www
.quiverfull.com/.

43. Alexander Burns, "Rick Perry's HPV [Human Papillomavirus Vaccine] Mandate Comes Back to Haunt Him," *Politico.com*,
September 13, 2011, http://www.politico.com/news/stories/
0911/63441.html.

44. Editorial, "'Safe Sex' for the Whole Nation: Why Man-
dating the HPV Vaccine Is Not a Good Idea," *Christianity Today*,

March 22, 2007, http://www.christianitytoday.com/ct/2007/april/18.26.html?start=1.

Chapter 9: *Obsession* versus *Jesus Camp*

1. William Safire, "On Language: Islamofascism Anyone?" *New York Times Magazine*, October 1, 2006, http://www.nytimes.com/2006/10/01/magazine/01wwln_safire.html?_r=0.

2. *Merriam-Webster's Collegiate Dictionary, Eleventh Edition* (Springfield, MA: Merriam Webster, 2003), 455.

3. Erik Ose, "Pro-McCain Group Dumping 28 Million Terror Scare DVDs in Swing States," *Huffington Post*, September 13, 2008, http://www.huffingtonpost.com/erik-ose/pro-mccain-group-dumping_b_125969.html.

4. This is a subjective description. Muslims' clothing is not monolithic, but it's safe to say that the man depicted in the film was not wearing bib overalls and a John Deere cap.

5. Daphna Berman, "*Obsession* Stokes Passions, Fears and Controversy," *Haaretz.com*, Thursday, June 22, 2007, http://www.haaretz.com/hasen/spages/873843.html.

6. The movie was initially released in 2006 but was widely distributed in 2008.

7. Meg Laughlin, "Senders of Islam Movie *Obsession* Tied to Jewish Charity," *Tampa Bay Times*, September 26, 2008, *tampabay.com*, October 2, 2008, http://www.tampabay.com/news/politics/national/article827910.ece.

8. CAIR, "Dr. Khaleel Muhammad Says: *Obsession* Film 'Vile Piece of Propaganda,'" *American Muslim*, September 28, 2008, http://theamericanmuslim.org/tam.php/features/articles/dr_khaleel_mohammed_says_obsession_film_vile_piece_of_propaganda/.

9. Chris Hedges, "The War against Tolerance," *Truthdig.com*, February 11, 2008, http://www.truthdig.com/report/item/20080211_the_war_against_tolerance.

10. See http://www.jesuscampthemovie.com/.

Chapter 10: Stealth Jihad

1. This quote is taken from ING's Web site, © 2011, http://ing.org/.

2. See http://www.ing.org/welcome-overview/13-ings-inception -and-early-history.

3. William Mayer, "Islamic Marketing 101—Maha ElGe-naidi of the Islamic Networks Group Takes Da'wa Act On The Road," *Militant Islamic Monitor*, April 22, 2008, http://www .militantislammonitor.org/article/id/3439.

4. Pew Research Center for the People and the Press, *Muslim Americans: Middle Class and Mostly Mainstream* (Washington, DC: Pew Research Center, 2007), summary posted and download of complete report offered, May 22, 2007, http://pewresearch.org/ pubs/483/muslim-americans.

5. Pew Research Center for the People and the Press, *Muslim Americans: No Signs of Growth in Alienation or Support for Extremism; Mainstream and Moderate Attitudes* (Washington, DC: Pew Research Center, 2011), *People-press.org*, August 30, 2011, http:// www.people-press.org/2011/08/30/muslim-americans-no-signs -of-growth-in-alienation-or-support-for-extremism/?src=prc -headline.

6. Mayer, "Islamic Marketing 101"; Beila Rabinowitz and William Mayer, "Islamic Networks Group—Dialogue as Da'wa," *PipeLineNews.org*, April 10, 2008, http://www.pipelinenews.org/ PipeIndexapril08.htm.

7. See Islamic Thinkers Society, "About Us," *IslamicThinkers .com*, August 19, 2004, http://www.islamicthinkers.com/index/ index.php?option=com_content&task=view&id=5&Itemid=57.

8. "About Robert Spencer," *Jihadwatch.org*, http://www .jihadwatch.org/about-robert-spencer.html.

9. See http://www.jihadwatch.org/why-jihad-watch.html.

10. See http://www.jihadwatch.org/2010/01/jihad-groups-set -up-camp-in-haiti.html.

11. See http://www.jihadwatch.org/2010/01/new-hampshire -federally-funded-program-for-somali-refugee-children-put-on -hold-after-charges-that-it.html.

12. Robert Spencer, *Stealth Jihad: How Radical Islam Is Subverting America without Guns or Bombs* (Washington, DC: Regency Publishing, 2008), 30.

13. Charles Burress, "Hindu Groups Lose Fight to Change Textbooks, but Decision by State Board of Education Is Supported by Some Hindu Americans," *San Francisco Chronicle*, March 10, 2006,

http://www.sfgate.com/cgi-bin/article.cgi?f=/c/a/2006/03/10/
BAGVSHK6JK63.DTL#ixzz0iIxjt7cE.

14. David Byrne, "The Limits of Multiculturalism," in David
Byrne's *Journal*, December 13, 2009, http://journal.davidbyrne
.com/2009/12/121309-the-limits-of-multiculturalism.html.

15. John L. Esposito, *What Everyone Needs to Know about Islam*
(New York: Oxford University Press, 2002), 164.

16. Spencer, *Stealth Jihad*, 14–15.

17. Mohamed Akram, aka. Mohamed Adlouni, wrote the
"Explanatory Memorandum," dated May 1991; a summary and
a downloadable PDF version in Arabic and English, dated May
22, 1991, are offered at http://www.investigativeproject.org/
document/id/20.

18. From page 4 (of 18, in the English part) of the PDF document in ibid., or see http://www.nefafoundation.org/miscellaneous/
HLF/Akram_GeneralStrategicGoal.pdf.

19. The text of "Stand Up, Stand Up for Jesus" was written by
George Duffield Jr. in 1858.

20. Spencer, *Stealth Jihad*, 7.

21. Ibid., chap. 3, "Silencing the Critics"; and chap. 4, "The
International Jihad against Free Speech."

22. Ibid, 124.

23. Ibid, 167.

24. Most observant Muslims consider usury to be a sin and are
reticent to lend or borrow money on interest. Banks that offer services in accordance with Islamic religious practice charge set fees
rather than compounding interest on money that is lent; money
deposited in such banks does not receive interest though often its
depositors benefit from investments that involve shared risk with
the bank. See Esposito, *What Everyone Needs to Know*, 167.

25. Ibid, 183.

26. Daniel Pipes, "A Madrassa Grows in Brooklyn," *New York
Sun*, April 24, 2007, http://www.nysun.com/foreign/madrassa
-grows-in-brooklyn/53060/.

27. Associated Press, "Arabic-themed NYC School Principal
Quits over Criticism of 'Intifada' T-shirts," *HaAretz.com*, August
11, 2007, http://www.haaretz.com/hasen/spages/892164.html.

28. Glenn Beck, "Is Sharia Law Gaining a Foothold in the
U.S.? America's Next Top Dead Models," *CNN.com*, transcript

of airing on March 27, 2007, http://transcripts.cnn.com/
TRANSCRIPTS/0703/27/gb.01.html.

29. Steve Rendall and Isabel Macdonald, "The Dirty Dozen:
Who's Who among America's Leading Islamophobes," *FAIR:
Fairness and Accuracy in Reporting*, October 1, 2008, http://www
.fair.org/index.php?page=3687.

30. See, e.g., http://www.premierchristiancruises.com/.

31. See   http://disneyworld.disney.go.com/parks/hollywood
-studios/special-events/night-of-joy/.

Conclusion: The Work Continues

1. Franklin Graham, in a letter accompanying *Decision* and
sent from Charlotte, NC, by the Billy Graham Evangelistic Association, April 2012.

INDEX

CPSIA information can be obtained at www.ICGtesting.com
Printed in the USA
BVOW03s1124150414

350636BV00001B/30/P